GROWING IN THE FRUIT OF THE SPIRIT

Bert Ghezzi and Peter Williamson
General Editors

Growing in the Fruit of the Spirit

John Blattner

SERVANT BOOKS
Ann Arbor, Michigan

Published by Servant Books
P.O. Box 8617
Ann Arbor, Michigan 48107

Printed in the United States of America
ISBN 0-89283-177-4

To my parents, whose cooperation with the Holy Spirit helped me grow as a son of God.

Contents

Living as a Christian

IN HUMAN TERMS, it is not easy to decide to follow Jesus Christ and to live our lives as Christians. Jesus requires that we surrender our selves to him, relinquish our aspirations for our lives, and submit our will to God. Men and women have never been able to do this easily; if we could, we wouldn't need a savior.

Once we accept the invitation and decide to follow Jesus, a new set of obstacles and problems assert themselves. We find that we are often ignorant about what God wants of us as his sons and daughters. For example, what does it mean practically to obey the first commandment—to love God with our whole mind, heart, and strength? How can we know God's will? How do we love people we don't like? How does being a Christian affect what we do with our time and money? What does it mean "to turn the other cheek?" In these areas—and many others—it is not easy to understand exactly what God wants.

Even when we do know what God wants, it can be quite difficult to apply his teaching to our daily lives. Questions abound. How do we find time to pray regularly? How do we repair a relationship with someone we have wronged or who has wronged us? How do we handle unruly emotional reactions? These are examples of perplexing questions about the application of Christian teaching to our daily lives.

Furthermore, we soon discover that Christians have enemies—the devil outside and the flesh within. Satan tempts us to sin; our inner urges welcome the temptation, and we find our will to resist steadily eroding.

Finally, we must overcome the world. We are trying to live in an environment that is hostile toward what Christians believe and how they live and friendly toward those who believe and do the opposite. The world in which we live works on our Christian resolve in many subtle ways. How much easier it is to think and act like those around us! How do we persevere?

There is a two-fold answer to these questions: To live successfully as Christians, we need both grace and wisdom. Both are freely available from the Lord to those who seek him.

As Christians we live by grace. The very life of God works in us as we try to understand God's teaching, apply it to our lives, and overcome the forces that would turn us aside from our chosen path. The grace we need is always there. The Lord is with us always, and the supply of his grace is inexhaustible.

Yet grace works with wisdom. Christians must *learn* a great deal about how to live according to

God's will. We must study God's word in scripture, listen to Christian teaching, and reflect on our own experience and the experience of others. Many Christians today lack this kind of wisdom. This is the need which the *Living as a Christian* series is designed to meet.

The book you are reading is part of a series of books intended to help Christians apply the teaching of scripture to their lives. The authors of *Living as a Christian* books are pastoral leaders who have given this teaching in programs of Christian formation in various Christian communities. The teaching has stood the test of time. It has already helped many people grow as faithful servants of the Lord. We decided it was time to make this teaching available in book form.

All the *Living as a Christian* books seek to meet the following criteria:

● **Biblical.** The teaching is rooted in scripture. The authors and editors maintain that scripture is the word of God, and that it ought to determine what Christians believe and how they live.

● **Practical.** The purpose of the series is to offer down-to-earth advice about living as a Christian.

● **Relevant.** The teaching is aimed at the needs we encounter in our daily lives—at home, in school, on the job, in our day-to-day relationships.

● **Brief and Readable.** We have designed the series for busy people from a wide variety of backgrounds. Each of the authors presents profound Christian truths as simply and clearly as possible, and illustrates those truths by examples drawn from personal experience.

● **Integrated.** The books in the series comprise a unified curriculum on Christian living. They do not present differing views, but rather they take a consistent approach.

The format of the series makes it suitable for both individual and group use. The books in *Living as a Christian* can be used in such group settings as Sunday school classes, adult education programs, prayer groups, classes for teen-agers, women's groups, and as a supplement to Bible study.

The *Living as a Christian* series is divided into several sets of books, each devoted to a different aspect of Christian living. This book, *Growing in the Fruit of the Spirit,* is part of a set that deals with Christian character. One of the goals of our Christian life is to become more like Jesus. We all know words, such as loving, meek, and joyful, that describe the qualities of Jesus. But we need help, not only in determining what these marks of character are but also in knowing how to grow in them. *Growing in the Fruit of the Spirit* and other books in this set define the elements of Christian character and teach Christians how to be transformed in the Lord's image and likeness.

The editors dedicate the *Living as a Christian* series to Christian men and women everywhere who have counted the cost and decided to follow Jesus Christ as his disciples.

Bert Ghezzi and Peter Williamson
General Editors

ONE

Christian Character

W E LIVE IN A "do it yourself" society. There is
practically no aspect of life that has not been
boiled down into a handful of quick, easy steps and
published in a paperback manual.

This mentality has even invaded our approach
to simply living as human beings. The next time
you are in a bookstore, look at the section marked
"psychology." There, just an aisle or two away
from the books on "How to Build Your Own
Patio" and "How to Install a Water Heater," are
literally hundreds of books with titles like "How to
Improve Your Personality," "How to Change
Your Life," "How to Become the Real You," and
so on. These books are—or at least purport to
be—"Do-It-Yourself Manuals" for character
growth. Becoming new men and women, they
imply, is simple. Just follow these six steps and . . .
presto!

Christians should know better. We know that
"who we are" is not something we determine, but
something God brings into being. Similarly, we
know that changing ourselves, though we do have
some part to play in it, must ultimately be the work
of the Lord.

It is easy to lose sight of this. Many of us, if we look closely, will often find ourselves taking a do-it-yourself approach to becoming better Christians, overcoming problems, changing, growing, improving.

The Fruit of the Spirit

This self-help approach is commonly taken when it comes to the fruit of the Spirit. Most of us are familiar with the scripture passage where this expression appears, Galatians 5:22-23. Many of us probably have it memorized:

But the fruit of the Spirit is love, joy, peace, patience, kindness, goodness, faithfulness, meekness, self-control.

Without quite realizing it, we read this passage as if it said, "The *fruits* of the Spirit *are* . . ." We tend to think of the qualities listed in the passage as separate and distinct, like presents under the Christmas tree: one labelled "joy," another "patience," and so on. In our minds they are "things" that we either "have" or else must somehow "get." After a quick inventory of ourselves, we conclude that we need to "get more" kindness, or self-control, or whatever.

Ultimately this approach misleads us. We begin to focus on the particular traits themselves, defining them, describing how they work, looking for a set of methods or techniques to acquire more of them.

It doesn't work, at least beyond a minimal level. The passage reads, "the *fruit* of the Spirit *is.* "It is in the singular, not the plural. Paul is talking, not about a batch of separate traits that exist and operate independently of one another, but about a single reality; not about a collection of fine jewels, but about different facets of the same gem: the fruit of the Spirit; what grows in us as a result of the Holy Spirit living within us; the kind of person we become as we grow to be more like Jesus.

This is the heart of the whole matter. Here is a definition of the fruit of the Spirit that can help us understand what Paul is talking about in Galatians 5: *The fruit of the Spirit is a life conformed to the character of Jesus Christ.* God's purpose is to make us like Jesus, and he has sent the Holy Spirit to dwell inside us in order to bring that about. If the Holy Spirit has his way, unhindered by our human limitations, he will make us just like God. That is the "fruit" of his work in us. The more successful the process is— the more we actually *do* become like Jesus—the more the fruit of the Spirit has been borne in our life.

Learning how to grow in the fruit of the Spirit, then, begins with learning more about what God is like. The more clearly we see what God is like, the more clearly we will see what we ourselves are supposed to be like, and the easier it will be for us to cooperate with the Holy Spirit.

My intention is to focus not so much on character traits as on a person—in fact, on three persons: God the Father, the Lord Jesus Christ, and the Holy Spirit: the three persons who are God. The type of question we will be asking throughout the book will be, not "How can we get more patience?" but, "How can we let the Holy Spirit make us more like Jesus, who *is* patience?"

What God Is Like

When we want to get to know a person, we ask the question, "What is he like?" This can be answered on a number of levels. We might describe the person physically: he is so many inches tall, weighs so many pounds, has this color eyes and hair, and so on. Going further, we might describe his personality: quiet and shy, boisterous and outgoing, humorous, pensive, or whatever.

But beyond that, we can describe his *character*. Here we come closer to what is most fundamental about him as a unique individual. When we know someone's physical description, we can pick him out in a crowded room; when we know his personality we can perhaps suggest an activity for the evening that will appeal to him. But when we understand his character, we can truly say that we know him: not just that we know things about him, but that we know *him*.

It is the same way when we want to get to know God. We can ask, "What is he like?" and get an answer. God, in this sense, is "like" something. He has certain qualities and traits and characteristics, and we can find out what they are. The more fully we understand them, the better we know God.

One of the main ways we find out what God is like is by looking at Jesus. John, in his gospel, says Jesus is "the word of God." That means that he is God's expression of himself. Jesus is also God's son: he shares God's nature in such a way and to such a degree that he can say, "He who has seen me has seen the Father" (Jn 14:9), and "I and the Father are one" (Jn 10:30).

Another way we can learn what God is like is by reading what he has said about himself in the Bible. In part, this consists of observing what he has done. For example, by seeing God perform a loving act we learn that he is a loving God. But beyond this, we learn what God is like because he tells us. Sometimes, someone in scripture asks God, "What are you like?" and God tells him. Other times the scriptural authors are simply inspired by the Holy Spirit to describe some aspect of God's character.

Galatians 5:22-23 is this kind of passage. It describes God, and in doing so it describes us as we will be when God has completed his work in us.

The same God who is so fully and definitively expressed in scripture and in the person of Jesus dwells in us in the person of the Holy Spirit. This is a familiar truth to us, perhaps, but it is worth appreciating what it means in the present context. It has everything to do with the fruit of the Spirit. Whenever we learn something about what God and Jesus are like, we should realize that that is also what the Holy Spirit within us is like, and that it is precisely what he is trying to make us like.

Our subject in this book will be Christian character. Character is a subject that does not get much attention these days, even among Christians. But it is a subject that is of vital importance, especially to Christians.

Our tendency is to focus on *gifts,* meaning either natural or the kind of spiritual abilities Paul mentions in Corinthians 12-14. But gifts are never exercised in a vacuum. Their fruitfulness is always a function of the character of the user.

Character is, in this sense, sort of a multiplier. It multiplies, for good or for ill, the effects of our gifts. Give a spiritual gift to a person of average character—let's rate it a one—and he is likely to exercise it in a responsible fashion. The same gift in the hands of someone with a much stronger and better-formed character—say, a five—will be five times more effective.

Of course, the principle works the other way around, too. You probably remember from high school mathematics that any figure multiplied by zero equals zero. Even an impressive and dramatic talent is wasted if the character of the person using it is weak. Then, of course, there are the "negative numbers." This reflects the harmful impact of a talented person using his gifts for distorted ends.

I have seen this principle manifested many times in the Christian life. I have seen people whose gifts were modest but whose character was sound do great things for God. I have seen others with spectacular spiritual gifts tragically ruined by weakness and flaws of character.

What is the point of all this? We all know that we have no control, no "say" over what gifts and talents come to us. That is precisely why we call them *gifts*. But we *do* have the ability, and therefore the duty, to develop our character, to grow in the fruit of the Spirit.

Because Galatians 5:22-23 is such a familiar passage, we could easily conclude that it is the only passage in scripture that describes the fruit of the Spirit, or that the particular qualities listed there are the only ones the Spirit is trying to develop in us.

Neither conclusion is true. There are in fact several passages in the New Testament that describe the kind of person we are meant to be. Here are some of the more prominent ones:

> I therefore, a prisoner for the Lord, beg you to lead a life worthy of the calling to which you have been called, with all lowliness and meekness, with patience, forbearing one another in love, eager to maintain the unity of the Spirit in the bond of peace. (Eph 4:1-3)

> Put on then, as God's chosen ones, holy and beloved, compassion, kindness, lowliness, meekness, and patience, forbearing one another and, if one has a complaint against another, forgiving

each other; as the Lord has forgiven you, so you must forgive. And above all these put on love. (Col 3:12-14)

But as for you, man of God . . . aim at righteousness, godliness, faith, love, steadfastness, gentleness. (1 Tm 6:11)

Finally, all of you, have unity of spirit, sympathy, love of the brethren, a tender heart and a humble mind. (1 Pt 3:8)

Make every effort to supplement your faith with virtue, and virtue with knowledge, and knowledge with self-control, and self-control with steadfastness, and steadfastness with godliness, and godliness with brotherly affection, and brotherly affection with love. (2 Pt 1:5-7)

Note that a number of character traits recur frequently in these passages, sometimes expressed by slightly different words. Here is a list of the most frequently mentioned qualities in these passages:
—love
—joy
—peace
—patience
—kindness
—generosity/goodness
—reliability/faithfulness
—gentleness/meekness
—self-control

—compassion
—lowliness
—zeal
—forbearance
—perseverance
—brotherly love

All these character traits—along with others mentioned in scripture—describe what God is like and what he wants us to be like. They are all "the fruit of the Spirit." Because Galatians 5:22-23 provides a good summary of them, we will use it in this book to outline our examination of the fruit of the Spirit. As may be obvious from the list above, sometimes different English words are used to describe the same trait, and many traits are closely related to each other. Therefore we will not be overly concerned with addressing each and every trait separately, and where two or more traits are closely related, we will cover them in the same context. For example, the chapter on love will also discuss kindness and goodness.

Chapters two and three will consider what it means for us to be made in the image and likeness of God. Chapters four through ten will examine some of the character traits of God, first to see what they look like in him and in his son Jesus, and then to consider how they are to look in us. We will conclude with a review of some basic principles of spiritual growth.

Let me suggest that as you read this book you keep your attention fixed on Jesus and not on yourself, your weaknesses, your limitations, the areas in which you need further growth. Read it, not as a "do-it-yourself" manual on spiritual growth, but as a guide to what the Lord himself is already doing in you. As we shall see, we *do* have a role to play in nurturing the fruit of the Spirit in our lives. But that role always has to do with cooperating with the work that the Holy Spirit is already doing in us: making us more like Jesus.

TWO

Children of God

THE FRUIT OF THE SPIRIT, as we have said, is a life conformed to the character of Jesus. We might also say it is *a life restored to the image and likeness of God*. As we shall see, God's original intent was that we be just like him, and that is still his goal for us. What he first set out to do through the original creation, he must now accomplish through the work of the Holy Spirit overcoming the effects of our sin. In this chapter and the next we will see how this is so, and the significance it has for our growth as Christians.

Sonship in Bible Times

We are going to begin with a passage from Luke's gospel that most of us probably do not read very often. It is Luke 3:23-38, a long list of the ancestors of Jesus.

"Jesus, when he began his ministry, was about thirty years of age, being the son (as was supposed) of Joseph, the son of Heli, the son of Matthat, the son of Levi. . . ." It is at about this point that most of us probably skip down to chapter four and resume reading. After all, scripture is full of genealogies; we have plowed through enough of them to know they are dull and uninteresting. The Jews may have been interested in their own ancestry, but we are not. Besides, we can't even pronounce most of the names.

But this particular genealogy ends in a rather unusual way, and if we skip over it we will miss an important bit of truth. Jesus, it says, was descended from "Cainan, the son of Enos, the son of Seth, the son of Adam, the son of God."

I can still recall being a bit startled the first time I read that last line and saw God's name included in the list so matter-of-factly. What does it mean? Certainly Adam was not God's son in the same way that Seth was Adam's son. How are we to interpret this statement?

When scriptural writers refer to someone as "the son of" someone (or something), they are often drawing an analogy that would have been clear to readers of their own era but that is lost upon us. In the times in which the New Testament was written, "sonship" implied something more than—and even something *other* than—mere biological descent.

A first-century reader would understand the term to refer to the total relationship that typically existed between a father and a son, especially a firstborn son. That relationship was much more minutely developed and culturally defined in those days than today. Unless we understand this relationship and grasp what it meant to be a son in first-century Jewish society, we will miss a great deal of what the scriptural writers were saying when they used the term "sonship."

A young boy in Jewish society was raised much differently than boys are raised today. Until the age of five or six, he was cared for almost entirely by his mother. At that age, he left the company of his mother and sisters and came under the direct and virtually exclusive care of his father. From that point on, he was his father's responsibility. In a very real sense, everything he would become as a man would result from the formative years spent as his father's disciple. According to the rabbis, it was his father's duty to teach him the laws of God, to establish him in an occupation, and to get him a wife. In short, it was his father's job to initiate him into full adult life.

During these years, the young boy would spend most of his time with his father. He would work with him, learning his father's occupation. Eventually he would succeed to his father's position in local society. He was his father's heir: everything his father had was his (see, for example, the parable of the prodigal son, Lk 15:31). He exercised his father's authority, and acted "on behalf of," or "in the place of," his father. When you related to the son, you were, in a certain sense, relating to the father (in this light, reread the parable of the vineyard, Mk 12:

Sonship constituted a man's very identity. This is reflected throughout the New Testament. When Jesus encounters Peter after the resurrection, he addresses him as "Peter, son of John" (Jn 21: 15-17). When the Nazareans marvel at Jesus' teaching, they ask, "Is not this the carpenter's son?" Nowadays people sometimes talk of "finding out who they are," but a son in Jewish society knew precisely who he was: he was the son of his father. It was an identity that shaped his entire life.

Each young boy was, in effect, a disciple of his father. As in all master-discipleship relationships, the goal was not merely for the disciple to learn some things from the master, but to become like him in almost every respect. It is not an overstatement to say that in Jewish culture a son was expected to grow up to become virtually a replica of his father.

This, then, is what it means to say that Adam was God's son: not that Adam was biologically descended from the Almighty, but that God related to him as a father related to his son. Thus, in Genesis we see God teaching Adam his law ("Of the tree of the knowledge of good and evil you shall not eat"), establishing him in an occupation ("Have dominion over the fish of the sea and over the birds of the air"), and even getting him a wife (by rather extraordinary means—Adam and Eve may be the only couple who were literally "made for each other").

Sonship in Adam

Not only was Adam, as an individual, created to be "the son of God" in this sense, but through Adam the entire human race was to enjoy the relationship with God characterized by the term "sonship."

The nineteenth chapter of Matthew's gospel records an incident in which the Pharisees challenge Jesus on the subject of divorce. The way Jesus answers their question is instructive, not only for what it teaches us about divorce, but for what it teaches us about how to understand the purpose of God for our lives.

> And Pharisees came up to him and tested him by asking, "Is it lawful to divorce one's wife for any cause?" He answered, "Have you not read that he who made them from the beginning made them male and female, and said, 'For this reason a man shall leave his father and mother and be joined to his wife, and the two shall become one flesh?' So they are no longer two but one flesh" (Mt 19:3-6).

The Pharisees' question had to do with an issue that was hotly debated in their day. Different rabbis held different positions on the subject. The Pharisees wanted to put Jesus on the spot by finding out where he stood on the controversy. But Jesus does not respond to them in those terms. In fact, he does not discuss the various current points of view at all. Instead, he refers to the original intention of "the one who made them from the beginning," and when he sets forth his position he quotes, not the words of any rabbi, but the words of God recorded in the book of Genesis.

Genesis is the book of origins. In it are recorded the beginnings of the human race and, more important for us, the purposes God had in mind in creating us. If we are to answer the most fundamental questions about who we are and what kind of people we should be, we will do well to follow Jesus' example and turn to the book of Genesis for guidance.

Genesis 1:26-28 recounts God's creation of the human race. It not only tells us *that* God created us and *how* God created us, it also tells us *why* God created us—the purpose he had in mind.

Then God said, "Let us make man in our image, after our likeness; and let them have dominion over the fish of the sea, and over the birds of the air, and over the cattle, and over all the earth, and over every creeping thing that creeps upon the earth." So God created man in his own image, in the image of God he created him; male and female he created them. And God blessed them, and God said to them, "Be fruitful and multiply, and fill the earth and subdue it; and have dominion over the fish of the sea and over the birds of the air and over every living thing that moves upon the earth."

In a moment we will return to the phrase "image and likeness," which the scriptural writer seems so determined to call to our attention. For now, notice the word "man." The Hebrew word translated here is *adam*. This was the generic term for man or mankind. It is also, of course, the word from which is derived the proper name Adam.

The term *adam* is translated differently in different places in Genesis. In Genesis 1:26, as we have just seen, it is rendered "man" in the sense of "mankind," or "the human race." In other places, such as Genesis 2:18, it is rendered "the man," denoting a particular individual who is a sort of prototype of the human race. And in still other places, such as Genesis 3:17, the same Hebrew word becomes the proper name of this individual.

Do you see the significance of all this? The story of Adam, with which we are all so familiar, is really the story not just of an individual, but of "man," of mankind, of the entire human race. What is true of this individual named Adam is true, in a broader sense, of the whole human race, and therefore of each one of us.

Now recall everything we said earlier about Adam being the son of God. Do you see the point? God wanted Adam to be his son, with all the depth and fullness of meaning that concept implies. By implication, then, it is clear that God wanted the whole human race, both individually and collectively, to be his son: to enjoy the kind of relationship with him that typified the relationship between a father and his son; ultimately, to become just like him.

This sonship, Genesis 1:27 says, involves our being created in "the image and likeness of God." This does not mean that we somehow bear a physical resemblance to God, or he to us. It means something far more significant: that we share God's *nature*. There is something of God within us; a sort of family resemblance.

No doubt you have heard people use the expression, "like father, like son." Often they are referring to unmistakable similarities in mannerisms or patterns of behavior that the father and son themselves may not be aware of. Sometimes, in fact, such similarities persist even when the son is trying his best to prove how *unlike* his father he is! It is like that with God and us. Even the most rebellious and blasphemous person reflects certain unmistakable similarities to his heavenly Father because in some basic way he shares God's nature: he was created in "the image and likeness" of God.

Genesis 1:26 and 1:28 also talk about mankind "having dominion" over nature. The significance of this is clearer to us now that we understand sonship. A son, we said, exercised his father's authority, acted on his behalf and in his stead. That is what Genesis is talking about here. Mankind, the son of God, was to exercise God's authority over the created universe, just as any son might be placed in authority over his father's affairs.

Sonship, then, is God's original purpose for us. It is what we were made for. It is what "he who made us from the beginning" had in mind. We were to be, each of us and all of us, sons and daughters of God.

(Before I go on, I need to take a moment to sort out a bit of possible confusion. So far I have been using exclusively the term "*son* of God," since the type of relationship alluded to was one that applied in Jewish culture only to sons and not to daughters. I do not mean to imply by this that only men can be "sons" of God. Such an assertion would contradict scripture. I hope it is obvious that women, too, are to enjoy this same kind of relationship. In the rest of this chapter and in the next chapter, I will refer to this type of relationship in terms of "sonship," since that is more true to the historical metaphor; but when I talk about those of us who enter into that relationship, I will usually speak of "sons and daughters of God," or of "children of God." Both usages refer to the same underlying spiritual reality.

Sonship in Christ

We all know, of course, what happened. Man fell. He turned his back on God, rejected his birthright, renounced his sonship. We are still "sons of God" in some sense; we still bear God's image and likeness. Yet the sonship we have received from Adam is fatally flawed. God needed a way to bring us back into the family, to restore us to his original purpose for us. That is where Jesus comes in.

Thus it is written, "The first man Adam became a living being"; the last Adam became a life-giving spirit. . . . The first man was from the earth, a man of dust; the second man is from

heaven. As was the man of dust, so are those
who are of the dust; and as is the man of heaven,
so are those who are of heaven. Just as we have
borne the image of the man of dust, we shall also
bear the image of the man of heaven.

(1 Cor 15:45, 47-49)

In this passage the apostle Paul summarizes the
difference between the sonship we inherit from
Adam and the sonship we obtain through Jesus
Christ. Jesus is "the second man," or the second
Adam. God, in his unspeakable love and mercy,
decided to overcome the effects of man's fall by
re-creating the human race according to his
original purpose. And he did it the same way as
before: through one man who is both the prototype and the beginning of a new race. In the first
creation it was Adam; in the second it is Jesus.

Jesus came to restore what God had intended to
do in the first place through Adam. God had
wanted Adam himself, and with him all mankind,
to be his son. He now sent Jesus to begin a new
mankind that could truly be his son, the body of
Christ.

For in Christ Jesus you are all sons of God,
through faith. (Gal 3:26)

But when the time had fully come, God sent
forth his Son, born of woman, born under the
law, to redeem those who were born under the
law, so that we might receive adoption as sons.

And because you are sons, God has sent the Spirit of his Son into our hearts, crying, "Abba! Father!" So through God you are no longer a slave but a son, and if a son then an heir.

(Gal 4:4-7)

In and through Jesus Christ, we are redeemed; we are adopted as sons; as sons we become heirs of our father and share in his nature; he gives us his Spirit to impart to us the same life that Jesus had and to enable us to live the life Jesus lived. In and through Jesus Christ we realize God's original purpose for us: we become sons and daughters of God.

THREE

Growing Up

VERY WELL, THEN, you say. I am a son or daughter of God. I am created in his image and likeness. Through faith in Jesus I am restored to the relationship God always desired to have with me; I have been "adopted" back into the family; I am destined to be a "replica" of my father in heaven.

Why, then, you ask, am I still the way I am? Why do I see so many obvious ways in which I am *not* like God? Why does a son or daughter of God still act the way I sometimes do? Being a child of God is nice, but surely there is more to it than this?

Indeed there is. Understanding the difference between the picture I painted in the last chapter of a son of God, and the all-too-evident reality that most of us experience in our daily lives, becomes easier if we simply recall the obvious fact that children start out as children and not as adults.

A few weeks ago my wife gave birth to our fourth child, a baby boy. Someday, I am sure, he will be a renowned preacher, President of the United States, and an All-Star major league shortstop, all at the same time. But at the moment he is—well, he is just a baby.

Don't get me wrong. Little Joseph is my son. In a certain sense he is as much my son as he possibly could be: his sonship is an historical and biological fact that can never be changed. If he packed up and moved away tomorrow and I never saw him again, he would still be my son. That is how sonship works.

But at the same time, there is a sense in which he is not yet fully "my son." This little fellow, who totally and completely shares my nature and enjoys the full and immutable status of being my son, can as yet do almost nothing that a son of John Blattner ought to be able to do. I can use a typewriter (sort of) and write books; he cannot even talk. I can drive a car and ice skate and play the piano; he cannot even walk. In fact, so far as I can tell, at this point in his young life he can do only four things: eat, sleep, cry, and—well, those of you who have ever changed a diaper will be able to guess what the fourth thing is.

What does Joseph lack? In one sense, nothing; in another sense, everything. He already possesses the raw material he needs to be my son, but he still needs to grow, to develop. He needs to be taught, to be trained, to be shown how. He needs to be brought to maturity.

It is the same with us. When we are born into God's family we become his sons and daughters, totally and completely. All the "raw material" we need to become just like him is available to us. But we are, in effect, still babies. We need to grow up spiritually. We must be raised to maturity.

What will this maturity look like? Paul, writing to the Galatians about his deep concern for their welfare, cries out, "My little children, with whom I am again in travail until Christ be formed in you!" (Gal 4:19). Why does Paul call the Galatians his children when they were actually grown men and women? We usually connect the concept of being a son or a daughter with being a little child. We think of sonship as something we grow out of, not something we grow into as we get older and more mature. But in biblical culture, sonship did not refer primarily to a period in one's life, but to a relationship that endured throughout life. It would not be uncommon for a sixty-year-old man, himself the father of a large family and well-established in the local community, still to be known primarily as the son of his father. Growing to maturity does not move us away from sonship but moves us more fully into sonship. That is what it means to be mature in the Christian life. It is to have Christ formed in us; to grow from "little children" into spiritual men and women in whom others can recognize the Lord himself.

How does this growth to maturity take place? There are many passages in scripture that describe the process. One is in Paul's letter to the Colossians:

> Do not lie to one another, seeing that you have put off the old nature with its practices and have put on the new nature, which is being renewed in knowledge after the image of its creator.

. . .Put on, then, as God's chosen ones, holy and beloved, compassion, meekness, and patience . . . (Col 3:9-10, 12)

Note the phrases, "the old nature" and "the new nature." The Greek word translated "nature" in both places could also be translated "humanity," or even "human." This reflects the creation of a new human race, as we discussed in the last chapter. We are to trade in our old humanity for the new humanity offered us in Christ.

The Part We Play

But note especially that it is an *active* process. We are to "put off" the old nature and "put on" the new. Paul does not say that God will do this in us, or that it will happen automatically: it is something *we must do*.

This putting off and putting on, moreover, involves what Paul calls "practices." All this talk about old and new natures and the re-creating of the human race can make the whole matter seem very ethereal and intangible. In fact it is quite the opposite. As far as *our* part is concerned, it is very practical and down-to-earth. Stop doing the things that correspond to the old nature, Paul says, and start doing the things that correspond to the new.

Another passage that illustrates what we are talking about comes from the Sermon on the Mount:

You have heard that it was said, "You shall love your neighbor and hate your enemy." But I say to you, Love your enemies and pray for those who persecute you, so that you may be sons of your Father who is in heaven". (Mt 5:43-45)

Notice again the active nature of our role. Jesus says *we must do* certain things *so that* we may be sons and daughters of God. When we first read this line, our response might be one of surprise, even a sort of indignation. "But I already *am* a son of God," we protest. "I don't need to do anything to become one. Jesus already did everything that needed to be done."

Of course that is true. But remember the point I made earlier about my son Joseph. He is indeed already my son, in the most important and basic sense. But there is another sense in which he becomes more fully "my son" as he grows up and learns to do things the way his father does them. In this passage, Jesus is talking not so much about our rebirth into God's family as about our growth to maturity. There is a very real way in which we do become God's sons and daughters as we learn how to act like him.

True Spirituality

Describing Christian maturity primarily in terms of conforming our outward behavior to God's standards does not, perhaps, sound terribly spiritual. It is worth pausing a moment to consider what we mean by the word "spiritual."

In his first letter to the Christians at Corinth, Paul writes:

> But I, brethren, could not address you as spiritual men, but as men of the flesh, as babes in Christ. I fed you with milk, not solid food; for you were not ready for it; and even yet you are not ready, for you are still of the flesh. For while there is jealousy and strife among you, are you not of the flesh, and behaving like ordinary men? (1 Cor 3:1-3)

The Corinthians, Paul says, were not "spiritual." To anyone who has read chapters 12-14 of this same letter, that must seem a very strange comment indeed. The Corinthians not spiritual? By some definitions of the term they were, if anything, *too* spiritual. They experienced the charismatic (we sometimes call them "spiritual") gifts in abundance. In fact, Corinth seems to have been the epicenter of a veritable charismatic earthquake, with prophecy, tongues, and the other gifts almost out of control.

But the real meaning of being spiritual, Paul seems to be saying, goes beyond being baptized in the Holy Spirit and exercising charismatic gifts. Being spiritual has something to do with the absence of jealousy and strife, with not being "of the flesh," with not "behaving like ordinary men." True spirituality, in other words, consists of living as God's sons and daughters, reflecting the character of Jesus.

Jesus himself said the same thing, in somewhat starker terms:

Not every one who says to me, "Lord, Lord," shall enter the kingdom of heaven. . . . On that day many will say to me, "Lord, Lord, did we not prophesy in your name, and cast out demons in your name, and do many mighty works in your name?" And then I will declare to them, "I never knew you; depart from me, you evildoers". (Mt 7:21-23)

Feelings vs. Behavior

All this brings us back to Galatians 5. So far we have spoken mainly of the latter part of this passage, which focuses on the fruit of the Spirit. But in our present context, we do well to consider the first part also:

Now the works of the flesh are plain: fornication, impurity, licentiousness, idolatry, sorcery, enmity, strife, jealousy, anger, selfishness, dissension, party spirit, envy, drunkenness, carousing, and the like. I warn you, as I warned you before, that those who do such things shall not inherit the kingdom of God. But the fruit of the Spirit is love, joy, peace, patience, kindness, goodness, faithfulness, gentleness, self-control. (Gal 5:19-23)

Paul here contrasts the fruit of the Spirit with what he calls "the works of the flesh." In some

ways this is the same point he was making in the
letter to the Corinthians, and the same point Jesus
made in the passage from Matthew's gospel: true
spirituality consists not in displays of charismatic
activity, but in a life of holiness.

But we can draw another lesson from Paul's
comparison, one that can save us considerable
confusion. It is this: the things listed as "the fruit
of the Spirit" are not feelings but *characteristic
ways of behaving.* Look again at the "works of the
flesh." They all have to do with behavior, with
relating to other people. They are bad things to *do,*
not bad *feelings.*

So it is with the fruit of the Spirit. Many people
equate the fruit of the Spirit with feelings. They
read Galatians 5:22-23 and ask themselves, "Do I
feel loving? Do I feel peaceful, or joyful, or kind?"
But that misses the point. Our emotions are
complicated, often misleading, and (contrary to
what our modern culture might suggest) strictly
secondary to living life as a son or daughter of
God. God is concerned not so much that we *feel*
loving as that we actually *love* one another.

As we turn now to examine the various character traits that Paul lists in Galatians 5:22-23,
bear in mind that our goal is not so much to see
those traits in and of themselves, but to see Jesus
through them, and thus to see ourselves as we will
be when the fruit of the Spirit comes to maturity in
our lives.

The fruit of the Spirit is a life conformed to the
character of Jesus Christ. It is the life of a son or

daughter of God who has been brought to maturity, in whom "Christ has been formed." It is the Spirit's work first of all, but we have an important role to play in it. We grow in the fruit of the Spirit by imitating God and his son Jesus; we are not focusing primarily on feeling a certain way but on acting a certain way, and so becoming more and more like Jesus.

FOUR

Love and Discipline

"The fruit of the Spirit is love, . . .
kindness, goodness. . ."

I AM SURE IT IS NO ACCIDENT that Paul's list of the character traits that identify the fruit of the Spirit begins with "love." Love, as Paul makes plain in his first letter to the Corinthians, is the preeminent Christian virtue:

> If I speak in the tongues of men and of angels, but have not love, I am a noisy gong or a clanging cymbal. And if I have prophetic powers, and understand all mysteries and all knowledge, and if I have all faith, so as to remove mountains, but have not love, I am nothing. If I give away all I have, and if I deliver my body to be burned, but have not love, I gain nothing. . . . So faith, hope, and love abide, these three; but the greatest of these is love.
> (1 Cor 13:1-3, 13)

Love is the preeminent virtue for Christians because it is the trait that most characterizes God.

I am sure you have heard it said many times that God is a God of love. This saying is familiar to us because it is so true. It was love that motivated God to create us, to sustain us in being, to make himself known to us, to sacrifice the life of his Son in order to buy us back from eternal death when we turned away from him. In short, as the apostle John says with such simplicity, "God *is* love," and because love is so central to his character, it must also be central to ours: "He who abides in love abides in God, and God abides in him" (1 Jn 4:16).

A God of Love

It is probably accurate to say that the entire Bible is an account of God's revelation of his love. Indeed, one of the things God seems most to want us to know and understand is love: his love for us, ours for him and for one another.

It certainly was one of the first things he tried to communicate to the Israelites. In chapters 32-34 of the book of Exodus we find the familiar incident of the golden calf. Let's take a moment to review these chapters. There are many lessons we could draw from them; for now, let's focus on what they tell us about God's love.

You know the basic outlines of the story: while Moses is away on Mount Sinai receiving God's law, Aaron and the people reject Yahweh and make themselves an idol, in the form of a golden calf. We all remember Moses' response: he shattered the tablets of the Ten Commandments in anger. What we may not remember or appreciate fully is *God's* response.

Simply put, God forgives them. He punishes those most responsible for the sin of the people—sin is never without consequences (more on that in a moment)—but he does *not* do precisely what the Israelites probably most feared he *would* do: he does not destroy them as a nation; he does not utterly abandon them.

It may be hard to see God's decision not to destroy the Israelites as an overwhelming sign of love and forgiveness. We might think it to be the *least* God could do! But the Israelites would not have seen it that way. Remember, you and I already know that God is loving and forgiving; they did not know that yet and had little reason to suspect it. All the nations that the Israelites came into contact with had their own "gods." Some were perhaps merely idols, others probably represented demonic powers. All were, quite simply, dreadful. Certainly no other "god" with whom the Israelites were familiar would have tolerated the kind of rebellion represented by the golden calf. Why would anyone expect this new God, Yahweh, to be any different?

But he *is* different, and that is one of the main messages of the entire story. In chapter 33, God answers Moses' prayer of intercession by renewing his promises to the Israelites and sending them on, once again, to take possession of the "land flowing with milk and honey." This time, however, there is one important difference. "But I will not go up among you," God adds, "lest I consume you in the way, for you are a stiff-necked people" (Ex 33:3).

Moses and the people are understandably distraught. They know that God's presence among them represents their only hope of success, their only protection from annihilation. But God makes it clear that he is withdrawing his presence *for their own good.* He knows that his holiness and justice will not mix with their sin and rebellion. If he remains among them, they will inevitably incur his wrath, and his justice will require that he punish them.

Moses immediately grasps what must happen. If God's chosen people are somehow incompatible with God, then the people must change; they must become more like God. But to do that, they must first know what he is like:

> Now therefore, I pray thee, if I have found favor in thy sight, show me now thy ways, that I may know thee and find favor in thy sight".
>
> (Ex 33:13)

By this point, Moses' prayer surely must ring a bell with us. We can restate his prayer in the terms we have been using in this book: "Father, if I am your son, teach me what you are like, so that I may truly become your son." Moses seeks what you and I seek: to grow in the fruit of the Spirit.

God grants Moses' request, and in the following

verses we find the account of the great theophany (self-revelation of God) on Mount Sinai. Read these verses carefully, for they are packed with information about God that is absolutely vital to us:

And he said, "I will make all my goodness pass before you, and will proclaim before you my name 'The Lord'; and I will be gracious to whom I will be gracious, and will show mercy to whom I will show mercy."

And the Lord descended in the cloud and stood with him there, and proclaimed the name of the Lord. The Lord passed before him, and proclaimed, "The Lord, the Lord, a God merciful and gracious, slow to anger, and abounding in steadfast love and faithfulness, keeping steadfast love for thousands, forgiving iniquity and transgression and sin, but who will by no means clear the guilty, visiting the iniquity of the fathers upon the children and the children's children, to the third and the fourth generation". (Ex 33:19, 34:5-7)

This is God's description of himself. He is saying to Moses (and to us): "This is what I am like. This is my nature. If you want to be like me and dwell in my presence, this is what you, too, must be like."

You have probably noticed how similar God's self-description here is to the passage in Galatians that describes the fruit of the Spirit. Many of the same qualities are listed in both places. What is noteworthy about the Exodus passage, however, is the focus on love. God is saying: "I am a God of love; my nature is to be loving." There are five words or phrases in this passage that are related to love. By examining each of them we can learn more about love as it is reflected in the character of God, and as it is supposed to be reflected in our character as his sons and daughters.

Goodness. God tells Moses, "I will make all my *goodness* pass before you" (Ex 33:19). When the Hebrew scriptures were first translated into Greek, the Hebrew word used here, *tub,* was often translated by two Greek words: *agathosune* and *chrestotes. Agathosune* is the word that in Galatians 5:22 is translated "goodness," and *chrestotes* is the word that is translated "kindness." So we are actually talking simultaneously about two of the character traits listed by Paul as the fruit of the Spirit.

In our own day, the word "good" is used as such a general term of approval that it often seems to have no meaning of its own at all. Here, we should understand "goodness" to mean "having the good of others at heart." To be good involves acting and speaking in such a way that the highest good of those around us is our highest priority. It is the opposite of malice, which means acting in order to harm others.

To say, then, that God is good means that he

loves us and has our best interest at heart in all he does. "We know that in everything God works for good [*agathos*] with those who love him, who are called according to his purpose" (Rom 8:28).

We, too, are to be *good*, to always act with the best interests of others at heart. In all our dealings with other people, we can ask ourselves a simple question: Is what I am about to say or do going to be for the highest good of this person?

Kindness. "Kindness" is very similar in meaning to "goodness," and seems equally difficult to define concretely. The Greek word, *chrestotes*, is sometimes translated "gentleness" or even, to add to the confusion, "goodness." But its root meaning has to do with appropriateness or helpfulness, as in a well-fitting yoke (see Mt 11:30) or a pleasing wine (see Lk 5:39). Thus, kindness means doing good to others (lending them money, doing favors for them), loving them by putting ourselves at their service. If goodness describes our *motive* in relating to others, kindness describes the things we *do* as a result of that motive.

Graciousness. "I will be gracious to whom I am gracious," the Lord told Moses. The Hebrew word translates into Greek as *charis*, which many of you will recognize as the root for "charism," or spiritual gift. William Barclay, in his book *New Testament Words,* defines *charis* this way:

The whole basic idea of the word is that of a free and undeserved gift, of something which comes from God's grace and which could never have been achieved or attained or possessed by a man's own effort.

One who is gracious is one whose nature is to give of himself in this way. The word *charis* is often translated "grace," as Barclay has indicated; sometimes it is rendered "favor." Perhaps the word we grasp most readily is "generosity."

Our God, then, is generous. He loves us freely. He loves us even though we do not deserve it, have no merit to make us worthy of it, can make no claim on it nor assert any right to it; he loves us, in fact, even though we continually spurn his love by our sinfulness.

Perhaps the most obvious and prominent manifestation of God's generosity is the mere fact that he unfailingly hears and answers our prayer. The Psalms are filled with testimonies to God's graciousness in hearing the prayers of his people:

Come and hear, all you who fear God,
and I will tell what he has done for me.

I cried aloud to him,
and he was extolled with my tongue.

If I had cherished iniquity in my heart,
the Lord would not have listened.

But truly God has listened;
he has given heed to the voice of my prayer.

Blessed be God,
>   because he has not rejected my prayer
>   or removed his steadfast love from me!
>   (Ps 66:16-20).

We know that whenever we pray we can expect God to hear us, because that is simply the kind of God he is. No one makes him answer us; no one could. He does it simply because it is his nature to do so. It is this aspect of God's character that inspired James to assure his readers, "Draw near to God and he will draw near to you" (Jas 4:8).

As we shall see in a moment, it is this quality of generosity, of grace or favor, that uniquely distinguishes Christian love as it is described in the New Testament. Sons and daughters of God are gracious or generous people who love not because others have earned it, but because it is their nature to be loving.

Merciful. God's love is marked by mercy. The scriptural word that is usually translated "mercy" is also sometimes translated "compassion," "pity," or even "tenderness." It means that God is moved by his people's needs.

Most of us, I suspect, would be somewhat suprised to encounter a mother or father whose care for their children was dry and without feeling. All of us have experienced the deep and powerful emotional bond that joins us to those we love, and we usually think of the parent-child relationship as the ultimate example of that bond. Scripture tells us that God loves us in just that way: "As a father pities his children, so the Lord pities those who fear him (Ps 103:13).

God's love for us is not merely mechanical, a dutiful response to a promise made long ago. He loves us with genuine feeling, with affection; the kind of love we see a father or mother exhibiting toward a child is simply a reflection of this aspect of God's character.

You have probably heard it said that you should not to confuse love with the mere feelings of infatuation, or affection, or sympathy. That is true. But it does not mean that our love is to be dry, sterile, and mechanical, devoid of feeling. Our emotions are not to be our masters, but neither are they to be our enemies. They are to be our servants, and they never serve us so well as when they enable us to love as God loves, with tenderness and compassion: with *mercy*.

Longsuffering. In describing himself to Moses, God says that he is "slow to anger." It is not hard to see how this relates to love: as Paul says, "Love is not irritable"; "it bears all things" (1 Cor 13:5, 7). We shall return to this concept in greater depth when we discuss patience, in chapter 7.

Steadfast Love. One of the most frequently mentioned characteristics of God is what the Old Testament calls "steadfast love." On Mount Sinai the Lord quite emphatically says that he is a God "abounding in steadfast love and faithfulness, keeping steadfast love for thousands" (Ex 34:6-7).

The Hebrew word used here, *chesed,* is one of the most majestic words in the Old Testament. It is used more than 100 times, translated into such English words and expressions as "loving kind- ness," "constant love" (in the proper sense: unwavering, unchangeable) "loyalty." A helpful way for us to grasp its meaning is to translate it "committed love" or "loyal care."

"Steadfast love" (it often appears with the word "faithfulness," to which it is closely related and to which we will devote an entire chapter) describes what God is like in relationships. When he has committed himself to a relationship, he is loyal to it; you can absolutely count on his love and care. It is the very essence of the kind of love he showed the Israelites in forgiving them and renewing his promises to them even when they rebelled against him. It is the quality in God that Paul referred to when he reminded Timothy that "if we are faithless, he remains faithful—for he cannot deny himself" (2 Tm 2:13).

Christian Love

So far, in discussing what Paul means by "love" in Galatians 5:22, we have focused on the way God described himself to Moses in Exodus 34:6-7. Now it is time for us to consider the word Paul actually uses in Galatians 5, *agape. Agape* sum- marizes, in one word, all that we have said about God's love, which must become ours as well.

"In this is love," John said, "not that we loved God but that he loved us and sent his Son to be the expiation for our sins" (1 Jn 4:10). *Agape* can be defined as the kind of love that motivated God to make the ultimate sacrifice: to become man for us, to suffer and die for us, so that we might be restored to fellowship with him. It is an unselfish love that gives of itself with no expectation of return.

It is crucial that we understand the New Testament concept of *agape*. Perhaps the most common English meaning of the word "love" is erotic, or romantic, love. In Greek this is expressed by the word *eros,* not by *agape.* Erotic love is based on an attraction for another person, often a sexually based attraction. This kind of love is exalted in our culture—in movies and books and popular songs—as the ultimate human relationship. *Eros* does sometimes contain a kind of unselfishness that is similar to the unselfishness in *agape,* but it is a selective unselfishness, bestowed only on the people one happens to be attracted to!

Our call as Christians is, first of all, to *agape,* to laying down our lives for others, even those to whom we do not find ourselves attracted. This is not to say there is anything wrong with *eros,* or that *eros* is somehow inherently incompatible with *agape.* The two can go together (and, in marriage for example, had better go together). But they *are* different, and *agape* takes precedence. It is *agape* that is the fruit of the Spirit.

Agape is the kind of love with which God loves us. It is the love by which Jesus laid down his life for us even "while we were yet sinners" (Rom 5:8).

It is a love that wants to do good for the other person, to serve him, to make him prosper (see 1 Cor 13:4-7). It is unconditional love, given as much to our enemies as to those who love us (see Lk 6:27-36). It derives not from what we see in the other person, but from the kind of person God has made us to be. It is not a stern, unpleasant duty, but something joyful, something we do from the heart, with affection and feeling—something we do because God has changed us into the kind of people whose nature it is to love.

God's Firmness

You may have thought it odd that I titled this chapter "Love and Discipline." At first glance the two may not seem to go together. In fact, however, they do; until we have understood the firmness with which God relates to us, we will not adequately understand his love.

As we have said, our God is a loving Father. But we must not make the mistake of thinking that he is indulgent or "soft-hearted" in the sense of being unconcerned about how we respond to his love. To use an expression that is commonly applied to some earthly parents, our God is not the kind of Father who "spoils" his children. There are very definite limits to what he allows, and discipline is an important part of how he relates to us.

Earlier, we discussed God's revelation of his love in Exodus 34. So far we have looked only at the first part of the passage, the part about goodness, graciousness, mercy, longsuffering, steadfastness, and the like. But there is a second part of the passage, and it is every bit as important to our study of love as the first part:

> . . . forgiving iniquity and transgression and sin, but who will by no means clear the guilty, visiting the iniquity of the fathers upon the children and the children's children, to the third and the fourth generation. (Ex 34:7)

It simply is not true that "anything goes" with God. We dare not confuse his forgiveness and slowness to anger with a kind of soft-headed benevolence. God's love and God's justice exist together, in a kind of tension: he does indeed love us, unutterably so, but there are limits to what he allows us to do, and consequences for us when we go beyond those limits.

Primarily, the consequence of stepping beyond God's boundaries is to taste the fruit of our own actions. It is not so much that God assesses a penalty for sin as that *sin is its own penalty.* Our sinful actions sow seeds of death and disorder, and it is we and our children and their children who will reap the cruel harvest.

How do we reconcile love and limits? The pattern is set by the Lord's treatment of the Israelites after they turned from him in the incident of the golden calf. God understands our fallen human nature. He knows that an "anything goes" approach on his part will inevitably lead to actions on our part that will prevent the very thing he most desires: a deep and full relationship of love between a father and his children. Thus it is precisely an act of love on his part to set limits, to establish boundaries, so that we can remain in fellowship with him. The circle is completed by his forgiveness, won for us on the cross by his Son Jesus Christ, and by which he restores us to fellowship with himself even when we overstep our bounds.

Discipline. Someone has said that in order to grow in the Christian life, you should read the parts of your Bible that you haven't underlined. That is good advice. Most of us readily become familiar with those passages of scripture that console us, excite us, bless us. We tend to skip over passages that challenge or convict us. I suspect one of the least underlined passages in the whole New Testament is Hebrews 12:5-11.

"My son, do not regard lightly the discipline of the Lord,
nor lose courage when you are punished by him.
For he disciplines him whom he loves,
and chastises every son whom he receives."
It is for discipline that you have to endure. God is treating you as sons; for what son is there whom his father does not discipline? If you are left without discipline, in which all have participated, then you are illegitimate children and not sons. Besides this, we have had earthly

fathers to discipline us and we respected them. Shall we not much more be subject to the Father of spirits and live? For they disciplined us for a short time at their pleasure, but he disciplines us for our good, that we may share his holiness. For the moment all discipline seems painful rather than pleasant; later it yields the peaceful fruit of righteousness to those who have been trained by it.

(Heb 12:5-11)

The first thing we must get clear is the meaning of the word "discipline." Most of us think immediately of spanking, or some other form of punishment. Discipline does include punishment, but that isn't all there is to it. The root word is "disciple." Discipline can be defined as everything a master does for his disciple to raise him up to be like himself. Try reading the passage above substituting the word "discipling" for "discipline."

The passage uses the metaphor of child-rearing. Parents will readily see that raising children involves much more than just spanking them when they misbehave. We teach them: what is right, what is wrong, how to read, why the sky is blue, why the grass is green, why this, why that, forever *why*. We train them: hold the fork like this, put your socks in that drawer, hem the skirt like this, mow the lawn this way. We correct them: no, you will need to add more yeast; no, you should release the clutch more slowly.

Teaching, training, correcting—this is what a master does for a disciple; this is what a father does for the son whom he loves; this is what our heavenly Father does for us, his children, "that we may share his holiness."

I was tempted to write that God's love is tempered by his discipline, but that is not quite right. God's love is *expressed in* his discipline. So should our love be. Our love for others should be expressed in a desire to see them grow in holiness and righteousness.

One time a friend of mine confided that he was in difficult financial straits and asked for my help and advice. He was behind in his rent and his utility payments; he was having trouble keeping food in the refrigerator. My first impulse was to give him some money and to discreetly ask a couple other friends to do the same. As I thought about it, however, I realized that bailing my friend out of the jam he was in was not really the best way to help him. He held a fairly good job; his problem was not lack of money but improper management of his money. Instead of offering him money, I volunteered to teach him how to use a budget.

I think I can safely say that our sessions together to discuss budgeting were rather painful for my friend. We uncovered a number of areas in which he had simply been irresponsible. It was difficult and a little embarrassing for him to agree to change his behavior.

I imagine there were times when he did not particularly *feel* "loved" by my insistence that he change some of his spending habits. But I believe the approach I took was really the best way to love my friend. In the end he was much better off than he would have been had I and some others simply given him money. I had, in effect, disciplined him; he had grown greatly in self-control and self-respect; financial shortages ceased to be a major problem for him.

Examples like this help us understand how to reconcile the apparent conflict between love and discipline. We cannot love too much, we cannot give too much, we cannot be too affectionate. We *can,* however, love in ways that are unhelpful, or at least "second-best."

It is a great grace both to give and receive discipline, whether from the Lord or from brothers and sisters in the Lord. It really helps us. It may, as the author of Hebrews said, seem painful rather than pleasant at the moment, but in the end it does indeed "yield the peaceful fruit of righteousness to those who have been trained by it."

The fruit of the Spirit is, first of all, love. It is the love we show one another, John tells us, that proves our ancestry, that shows we are truly sons and daughters of God. It cost God a great deal to restore us to himself, to be a God of grace who brings salvation: we, too, will find that it costs us to be men and women who lay down our lives in love for one another.

Beloved, let us love one another; for love is of God, and he who loves is born of God and knows God. He who does not love does not know God; for God is love. In this the love of God was made manifest among us, that God sent his only Son into the world, so that we might live through him. In this is love, not that we loved God but that he loved us and sent his Son to be the expiation for our sins. Beloved, if God so loved us, we also ought to love one another. No man has ever seen God; if we love one another, God abides in us and his love is perfected in us. (1 Jn 4:7-12)

FIVE

Rejoice!

The fruit of the Spirit is . . . joy.

MOST OF US, I THINK, find it difficult to picture Jesus as a genuine, flesh-and-blood human being. All our lives we have seen him portrayed as an austere figure in stained-glass windows and religious paintings. In these depictions Jesus seldom smiles, much less laughs; he never frowns unless he is exercising judgment; he is never seen relaxing, conversing amiably with friends, greeting others with a warm embrace. Instead he is portrayed as "holy": somewhat detached, aloof, almost other-worldly. The ethereal halo of light that surrounds his head only adds to the effect.

It is easy to sympathize with the motives of the artists who render these portrayals of Jesus. He is, after all, God-become-man. As such he is unlike any other person who has ever lived; we do well not to become overly-casual about him. It is perfectly right for us to relate to Jesus with the utmost respect.

Even so, we should not let ourselves lose sight of his humanness. Remember that the Incarnation has two aspects. "In him all the fullness of God was pleased to dwell," it is true, and by looking at Jesus we see clearly what God is like. But it is also true that Jesus is fully man, and part of the glory of the Incarnation is that in Jesus we can see humanity as it was meant to be. Actually, it is suprising to see how often the gospels show Jesus "acting like a normal person." He displays authentic human responses to typical human situations.

For example, he rejoices at good news. When the seventy disciples reported their success in carrying out the mission Jesus had entrusted to them, Luke says that Jesus "*rejoiced* in the Holy Spirit" (Lk 10:21). How do you picture this scene? Do you see Jesus solemnly lifting his eyes toward heaven with a transported gaze, uttering a stately psalm of thanksgiving? The word Luke uses can actually be translated "jumped for joy." Try reading the passage that way: "In that same hour Jesus jumped for joy in the Holy Spirit." You may never have imagined Jesus jumping for joy, but that is what Luke says he did.

Jesus also experienced sorrow: "And when he drew near and saw the city he *wept* over it" (Lk 19:41). When a leper approached him and asked Jesus to heal him, Mark notes that Jesus was "moved with *pity*" (Mk 1:41). When the Pharisees balked at him healing the man with the withered hand, "he looked at them with *anger, grieved* at their hardness of heart" (Mk 3:5). When he contemplated his imminent betrayal, suffering, and death, John says, "he was *troubled in spirit*" (Jn 13:21). Joy, sorrow, compassion, anger: in any number of situations, we see the Christ who was truly man respond in a natural, authentic human manner.

Emotions As Servants

Sometimes Christians have made the mistake of thinking that they should somehow rise above their emotions, like the ancient Stoics. But Christianity has never been opposed to human feelings. Our emotions were created by God; they were part of what he saw in us when he proclaimed his creation "very good."As we grow in maturity in our Christian life, we should find our emotions helping us respond properly to God's grace rather than disappearing or ceasing to influence us.

Many Christians today seem to be less in danger of becoming stoics than of being dominated by their emotions. Our feelings, we are told, represent our true identity; they are our surest guides to self-realization and authentic behavior. Far from despising or repressing our emotions, we are encouraged to focus on them, to stir them up, to give them free reign in our lives.

We have already discussed how this distorted view of the role of emotions can cause confusion when we try to understand the fruit of the Spirit. We tend to see the list of character traits in Galatians 5:22-23 as emotions that the Holy Spirit will produce in us. Thus we find ourselves worrying about whether we *feel* loving, or peaceful, or joyful, rather than whether our thoughts, speech, and actions are in accord with the character of Jesus.

God does not want us to be afraid of our emotions, nor does he want us to be dominated by them. Rather, he wants our emotions to serve us the way they served Jesus, by becoming a natural and spontaneous part of an authentic human response to situations that confront us.

This means that we ought to experience the right emotion at the right time. Paul, writing to the Corinthians, said that love "does not rejoice at wrong, but rejoices in the right" (1 Cor 13:6). Love *rejoices*—emotion plays a part—but it rejoices in the right way, at the right time, for the right reason. The obvious inference is that rejoicing will be out of place in some situations. As we grow to maturity as children of God, we will find our emotions becoming increasingly integrated into an *appropriate* response to a given situation.

The Right Response

All this theory of how our emotions should work looks good on paper, but how can we get it to happen in real life? Granted, it would be nice if we always experienced the right emotion at the right time, but how can we help what we feel? Feelings are things we either have or don't have. Some days we feel happy and other days we feel sad and we don't really know why we feel the way we do. How can we gain control over our feelings?

We need first to understand a subtle but important distinction concerning our emotions. The distinction is between *reaction* and *response*. A reaction is what happens inside us apart from our control: someone insults us and, without thinking about it or deciding to do it, we get angry. A response is what we decide to do with our reaction: ignore the insult, perhaps—or, alternatively, punch the other person in the nose.

Usually we tend to think that the reaction determines the response: I feel angry, and so I either respond in anger or I overcome the anger and remain calm; I feel afraid, and so I either run away or overcome the fear and stay put. But it can also work the other way around: our response can shape our reaction. By deciding to act calmly I begin to feel calm; by deciding to act bravely I begin to feel courageous.

It works the same way with joy; in fact, that is what Paul was talking about in 1 Corinthians 13:6. He did not say love was supposed to "feel happy" at the right and "feel unhappy" at the wrong. He talked not about our reaction but about our response: we are to "rejoice" in the right. "Rejoice" is an active verb, it is something we *do*. As we consistently rejoice in the right, we will find in time that we also come to "feel happy" in it, too. Our reaction will be shaped by our response.

Sorrow Responding to Pain

Interestingly enough, we can see this principle at work most clearly in some scriptural examples having to do with sorrow. Sorrow, grief, mourning: these are responses to pain or misfortune.

They are the opposite of joy. Now, many Christians, who have heard that they are supposed to be "joyful," conclude that they are never supposed to be sorrowful: that grief or mourning are somehow incompatible with being a Christian. But this is not the case.

In the eleventh chapter of his gospel the apostle John tells the story of the raising of Lazarus. Jesus, you recall, has been summoned to Lazarus' sickbed, but by the time he arrives Lazarus has died.

> When Jesus saw her [Mary] weeping, and the Jews who came with her also weeping, he was deeply moved in spirit and troubled; and he said, "Where have you laid him?" They said to him, "Lord, come and see." Jesus wept.
>
> (Jn 11:33-35)

Jesus wept. We have already seen other instances in which Jesus displayed the whole gamut of human emotions, so we are not particularly surprised to see him weep. His friend is dead; naturally he is sorrowful.

And yet . . . look back to the beginning of the story:

> He said to them, "Our friend Lazarus has fallen asleep, but I go to awaken him out of sleep." The disciples said to him, "Lord, if he has fallen asleep, he will recover." Now Jesus had spoken of his death, but they thought that he meant

taking rest in sleep. Then Jesus told them plainly, "Lazarus is dead; and for your sake I am glad that I was not there, so that you may believe". (Jn 11:11-15)

Long before he arrived at Bethany, long before he saw Mary and the Jews weeping, Jesus knew that Lazarus was dead. Not only that, he also knew that he was going to raise Lazarus from death. And yet he wept. Why? It seems odd to weep for a friend several days after you know of his death; it seems positively absurd to do so when you know he is going to come back to life. Why, then, did Jesus weep?

He wept because sorrow, at the human level, is an appropriate response to pain, and the death of a loved one—even when it is to be reversed—is painful. Even when death is destined to be overcome, death still represents a victory, however short-lived, for sin and the power of darkness. It still deprives us of the presence of a loved one. Mary and the Jews felt this keenly; Jesus, in spite of what he knew lay in store, felt the same pain and responded to it as they did.

I might point out, in passing, that this example is quite relevant to the way we as Christians respond to death. We often try to approach funerals as joyous occasions. After all, our Christian friends who die are destined to be raised from death just as surely as Lazarus was (not to mention, just as surely as Jesus was!), and our certainty is no less real than Jesus' certainty about Lazarus.

But something is missing in this approach, and we usually sense it. For all our joy about the resurrection to come, we still experience the pain of loss and separation, and it is appropriate to respond to this pain with grief and mourning. Paul taught the Romans, "Rejoice with those who rejoice, weep with those who weep" (Rom 12:15). That is what Jesus was doing in John 11, and it is right for us to do the same.

Rejoice!

Just as mourning is an appropriate response to misfortune, rejoicing is an appropriate response to good fortune.

What man of you, having a hundred sheep, if he has lost one of them, does not leave the ninety-nine in the wilderness, and go after the one which is lost, until he finds it? And when he has found it, he lays it on his shoulders, rejoicing. And when he comes home, he calls together his friends and his neighbors, saying to them, "Rejoice with me, for I have found my sheep which was lost". (Lk 15:4-6)

Notice, again, that rejoicing is an active response, not just an emotional reaction. Now, when the shepherd first finds the lost sheep he probably does feel joyful. But the shepherd does not go to his friends and say, "Feel happy with me." He says, "Rejoice with me!" It is as if he were saying, "Come to my house for a party! Celebrate my good fortune with me!"

Sometimes it is right for us to respond in joy even when our reaction is totally contrary. In the book of Nehemiah we are told of the rediscovery of the law of God by the returning exiles, who have not had access to it for several generations. Upon hearing it, they realize that they have unwittingly been disobeying the law for many years and are struck with remorse for their sin: "For all the people wept when they heard the words of the law" (Neh 8:9).

Now this may seem to us a very commendable reaction, and in many ways it was. As it happened, however, the day on which the reading of the law took place was the Feast of Tabernacles—a day on which the Israelites were supposed to celebrate and make merry.

And Nehemiah, who was the governor, and Ezra the priest and scribe, and the Levites who taught the people said to all the people, "This day is holy to the Lord your God; do not mourn or weep. . . . Go your way, eat the fat and drink the sweet wine and send portions to him for whom nothing is prepared; for this day is holy to our Lord; and do not be grieved, for the joy of the Lord is your strength." . . . And all the people went their way to eat and drink and to send portions and to make great rejoicing, because they had understood the words that were declared to them". (Neh 8:9-10, 11)

Nehemiah did not merely tell the people to *feel* differently. Their rejoicing was active; it was something they *did*, making use of familiar customs of celebration.

This same principle can be of great use to us as Christians. For many years I was somewhat troubled by my own experience of Easter. I knew Easter was the greatest and most glorious day of the year; I knew it commemorated the most stupendous event in the history of the world; I thought I should experience it as one of the most exciting and exhilarating days of the year.

It seldom was. For one reason or another, Easter always turned out to be pretty much like most other Sundays. In fact, sometimes I worked so hard at feeling exhilarated on Easter that I would become a little depressed by how ordinary I actually felt! Of course the problem was that I was focusing on my feelings, on my reaction, rather than on the proper response. I have since found that I do better to stop trying to "feel joyful" on Easter. Instead, I concentrate on celebrating it in the ways I know are appropriate—attending church, inviting friends and family for a fancy meal, singing favorite resurrection hymns—and am much better able to rejoice in the resurrection and to enter into the full experience of Easter.

The Joyful Christian

So far we have been discussing rejoicing as an active response which we make to particular situations. But the joy that is the fruit of the Spirit goes beyond this. This kind of joy is an abiding character trait, something that is to characterize us at all times. Paul was quite emphatic on this point:

> Rejoice in the Lord always; again I will say, Rejoice. Let all men know your forbearance. The Lord is at hand. (Phil 4:4-5)

> Rejoice always, pray constantly, give thanks in all circumstances; for this is the will of God in Christ Jesus for you. (1 Thes 5:16-18)

> Rejoice in your hope, be patient in tribulation, be constant in prayer. (Rom 12:12)

James tells us that we are even to rejoice when we are undergoing difficulties:

> Count it all joy, my brethren, when you meet various trials, for you know that the testing of your faith produces steadfastness. (Jas 1:2)

By this point we may be tempted to ask, as Nicodemus once did, "How can these things be?" What does it mean to be joyful at all times? How can we rejoice in all circumstances when we are also supposed to grieve in appropriate situations?

To begin with, the joy that is to characterize us is not something we muster up. It comes from the work of the Holy Spirit. "The kingdom of God is not meat and drink," Paul observed, "but righteousness and peace and joy *in the Holy Spirit*" (Rom 14:17). This is, after all, what it means to say that joy is the fruit of the Spirit.

Beyond this, we can be people who always rejoice because we are people whose fundamental situation is good. We are in Christ. We are restored to fellowship with God. We are temples of the Holy Spirit. Our eternal destiny is secure and glorious, and our joy is simply an unchanging response to these unchanging truths. Paul told the Philippians to rejoice because "the Lord is at hand." He told the Romans to rejoice "in your hope." Our joy is always based on the truth. In individual situations, it is based on the truth that the particular circumstances are good; as a general characteristic it is based on the truth that our fundamental situation is good.

This is why James can tell us to rejoice even in trials: not because the trials themselves are enjoyable, but because of what they produce in us. Besides, no matter how unpleasant our present circumstances, we can always rejoice in our unshakable hope.

I believe the Lord wants us to learn how to call upon these fundamental truths and rejoice in them. Feeling down? Rejoice, son of God! The joy of the Lord is your strength! Screaming children getting on your nerves? Rejoice, daughter of God! The Holy Spirit lives in your heart! Short of funds? Rejoice, child of God! Your reward is great in heaven!

The fruit of the Spirit is joy. As we learn to recognize the truth of our circumstances and respond to them with rejoicing, the Holy Spirit within us will be free to change us and make us into joy-filled people.

SIX

A Place for Everything . . .

The fruit of the Spirit is . . . peace.

DAN IS AN AGENT for an insurance company. He
enjoys his work, but today he arrives at the office
in a sour mood. In fact, he has been annoyed all
week, and he knows the reason: his fellow agent,
Ray, who shares the office with him. Ray is a
member of Dan's church. He is a good agent who
brings in a lot of business, but he is not an easy
person to share an office with. This morning, Dan
notices, Ray has left file folders strewn across his
desk, along with an empty pop bottle and the
wrapper from a vending-machine sweet roll.
Grumbling to himself, Dan puts away the empty
bottle and tosses the wrapper in the wastebasket.
He begins to straighten up and put away Ray's
files, a familiar but nonetheless irritating task.

A distinct chill has settled over the family room
where Don and Gloria are discussing their fi-
nances. Don is riffling through the month's bills,
fretting out loud about where the money to pay
them is going to come from. Don makes a good
income, and Gloria does her best to be frugal, but

they never seem to have enough money. Well . . . almost never. Last month, Gloria remembers, there seemed to be enough to buy new tires for the station wagon. But this month, when there is a sale on wallpaper that would make the upstairs bathroom presentable, things are "too tight." Gloria asks about the wallpaper again and Bill wearily points to the present balance in the checkbook. Maybe next week, he says, or maybe next month. He sighs. Gloria just doesn't seem to have a head for figures.

Tom is a mystery to his friends. He is cheerful and outgoing, always quick to suggest a get-together or to promise to drop by and help with a work project. He is energetic and successful in his work as a salesman. The puzzling thing is that few of the activities he suggests ever take place. At the last minute he always seems to remember a prior engagement or to find himself swamped with work. One Saturday morning he called around the neighborhood and arranged a tennis game for that afternoon; then he took a nap and slept right through it. His friends have learned to take his promises with a grain of salt, but they still find him exasperating. Tom, for his part, doesn't understand why life always seems so hectic.

Emily is somewhat frazzled as she climbs behind the wheel of the family car. She is right in the middle of making dessert for tonight's Bible study and needs more sugar. She could borrow a cup from Sally, but she and Sally aren't on very good terms right now. Something Emily said after church on Sunday offended Sally, though it didn't seem like such a big deal to Emily. Oh well—these things happen from time to time, she reminds herself as she pulls into the grocery store parking lot. Sooner or later they blow over. Emily just hopes this particular incident blows over before Sally and her husband arrive for tonight's Bible study.

I suspect all of us know someone like the fictional characters I have described here. Perhaps some of us even recognize ourselves in one or another of them! The situations are common ones, among Christians no less than among other folks. We might attribute each of these episodes to a variety of different problems. But a common thread runs through all the vignettes: each illustrates a situation in which there is a lack of *peace*.

I do not mean simply that the individuals involved feel ill at ease about what is happening. No doubt that is true, but how they are feeling is not the point. Peace, as Paul uses the term in Galatians 5:22, does not refer simply to the subjective state of feeling calm and free of anxiety. It is an objective condition that exists apart from how we happen to be feeling at the moment.

The term *peace* is used in scripture to refer mainly to three things: a right relationship with God, right relationships with others, and order in our personal life. As we shall see, these three are interwoven with one another.

Peace with God

> Therefore, since we are justified by faith, we
> have peace with God through our Lord Jesus
> Christ. (Rom 5:1)

To say that we have peace with God is more
than to say that we feel comfortable in his
presence. It means that we, who once were
"estranged and hostile in mind, doing evil deeds"
(Col 1:21), who by our sinfulness and refusal to
submit to his law made ourselves "enemies of
God" (Rom 11:28), have been reconciled to him
and restored to fellowship with him. Once we were
at war with God; by his death on the cross Jesus
has made it possible for the hostilities to cease, for
us to be God's friends—even his children—and
not his enemies.

In one sense, this kind of peace is not something
we grow in, but something we simply have: we are
reconciled to God, once and for all, by the cross of
Christ; it is an accomplished fact. There is another
sense, though, in which we do grow in peace with
God. The more clearly we see God's ways and
walk in them, the more we appropriate his power
to live as his sons and daughters, the more
faithfully we seek his forgiveness when we fail, the
more the spiritual reality of our right relationship
with God becomes an experiential reality. In this
sense, peace with God is indeed a fruit of the
Spirit: as we grow to maturity as children of God,
we experience more and more the blessings and
benefits of living in his kingdom.

Right Relationships

When Jesus died on the cross, he did more than make it possible for us to be reconciled to God. He also made it possible for us to be reconciled to one another.

> But now in Christ Jesus you who once were far off have been brought near in the blood of Christ. For he is our peace, who has made us both one, and has broken down the dividing wall of hostility, by abolishing in his flesh the law of commandments and ordinances, that he might create in himself one new man in place of the two, so making peace, and might reconcile us both to God in one body through the cross, thereby bringing the hostility to an end.
>
> (Eph 2:13-16)

Jesus did not address only the enmity between man and God; he also addressed the "dividing wall of hostility" between man and man. Part of his purpose was to reconcile us to one another, to create "one new man," to bring us together "in one body."

What we said about peace with God is also true of peace with one another. It is an already-existing spiritual reality, but it is also something we grow in at the natural level. Most of us know from personal experience that our relationships with others often fall short of the ideal of unity presented in scripture. Part of growing in peace involves learning how to make our relationships

with others work more smoothly. Paul offers some
excellent advice in his letter to the Colossians:

> *Put on,* then, as God's chosen ones, holy and
> beloved, *compassion, kindness, lowliness, meek-
> ness,* and *patience, forbearing* one another and, if
> one has a complaint against another, *forgiving*
> each other; as the Lord has forgiven you, so you
> also must forgive. And above all these put on
> *love,* which binds everything together in perfect
> harmony. And let the *peace* of Christ rule in
> your hearts, to which indeed you were called *in
> the one body.* And be *thankful.* (Col 3:12-15)

This passage is something of a primer on how
Christian personal relationships can flourish. The
goal, Paul says, is that peace characterize our
relationships "in the one body." In order for this
to happen, though, there are some things we must
do.

First, we must "put on" certain character traits.
We recognize some familiar words. Love, compassion, and kindness were discussed in chapter four.
Lowliness and meekness have to do with placing
ourselves at the service of one another; we will talk
more about them in chapter nine. Thankfulness,
as used here, is similar to joy as we discussed it in
the last chapter: a deliberate response to something good that someone has done for us. Patience
we will consider at length in the next chapter.

In addition to "putting on" these various
qualities, Paul mentions two other things we must

do. We must "forbear," and we must "forgive."
These are two essential skills for building and
sustaining strong, loving relationships.

To "forbear" means to put up with things that
may irritate us but are not wrong in themselves.
You know, of course, that people are always doing
irritating things. They always turn on the radio in
the morning carpool when you would rather read
the newspaper in silence. They always tell jokes
that you do not think are funny. They always walk
off with the sports section so that it is never there
when you are ready to read it. They eat supper half
an hour before you do, so that their children are
always knocking on the door just as you are saying
grace. I am sure you can add to the list.

What are we to do about all these irritants? In
some instances we might mention our difficulty,
and the other person might willingly change his
behavior to avoid bothering us. Most of the time,
though, we should simply forbear. Love, Paul told
the Corinthians, "does not insist on its own way"
(1 Cor 13:5). As long as we are dealing with
behavior that is not sinful, forbearance is usually
the best course.

But what about behavior that *is* sinful? Sometimes we are irritated by things other people do for
the very good reason that what they are doing is
wrong! Then what do we do?

Primarily, we forgive them. "As the Lord has
forgiven you, so you must also forgive." Not
grudgingly, not reluctantly, not only after we have
made them feel bad for hurting us. Our funda-

mental disposition is to be forgiving.

Forgiving others for wronging us often pre-supposes that we have called the wrongdoing to their attention. We have already made the point that love is sometimes best expressed through discipline. Often the most loving thing we can do for a brother or sister is to correct them, so that they can avoid further wrongdoing in the future. Correcting someone does not involve being judg-mental and overbearing; rather, we should act out of a desire to see the other person grow in holiness and to see our relationship restored. "If your brother sins against you, go and tell him his fault, between you and him alone. If he listens to you, you have gained your brother" (Mt 18:15).

Of course, if we are going to correct others, we should be all the more eager to correct our own wrongdoing. Any time we know we have wronged someone, we should be ready to admit our wrong action, resolve not to repeat it, ask forgiveness of the Lord and of the person we have wronged, and make restitution for our actions whenever that is appropriate.

If you are offering your gift at the altar, and there remember that your brother has some-thing against you, leave your gift there before the altar and go; first be reconciled to your brother, and then come and offer your gift.

(Mt 5:23-24)

Note that when our brother has done wrong, we should go to him; when *we* have done wrong, it is still we who should take the initiative to resolve the problem. The point is clear: broken relationships must be a very high priority for us. No matter who may be at fault, we have the responsibility to do whatever we can to make the relationship right again. "If possible, so far as it depends upon you, live peaceably with all" (Rom 12:18).

In this context we can begin to see how the vignettes at the start of the chapter illustrate lack of peace in personal relationships. Take Don and Ray, the office-mates. Ray could certainly help matters by keeping his desk tidy. It might be a good idea for Don to call the problem to his attention: with neater work habits, Ray might well become a more efficient worker. At the same time, it is not sinful to leave a desk untidy. Don could make his relationship with Ray more peaceful simply by learning to forbear Ray's irritating habit.

The relationship between Emily and Sally has been harmed by some wrongdoing on Emily's part. Waiting for it to "blow over" doesn't solve anything; it just sets the stage for a bigger storm next time. Emily needs to go to Sally and say, "What I said to you the other day was unkind. I didn't really mean it, of course, but I do need to work harder at controlling my tongue. Will you forgive me?" Or Sally could take the initiative and say to Emily, "I know you probably didn't mean what you said the other day, but your words really upset me. Can we talk about it and get it resolved? I don't want our friendship to suffer." Either approach should lead to Emily asking for and receiving forgiveness, and to a restoration of peace in a broken relationship.

Order in Our Personal Life

A third meaning of "peace" is suggested by a line in Paul's instructions to the Corinthians about the use of charismatic gifts in worship. The church at Corinth had a problem with what might be called charismatic chaos: people were praying, prophesying, speaking and interpreting messages in tongues, all at the same time. Paul's advice sounds remarkably like a teacher speaking to a classroom full of unruly third-graders:

> If any speak in a tongue, let there be two or at most three, and each in turn. . . . Let two or three prophets speak, and let the others weigh what is said. If a revelation is made to another sitting by, let the first be silent. For you can all prophesy one by one. . . . For God is not a God of confusion but of peace.
>
> (1 Cor 14:27, 29-31, 33)

Peace, Paul says (it is the same Greek word he uses in Galatians 5:22) is the opposite of confusion. A good word for it is *order*.

To many people *order* is a slightly distasteful word. It sounds too much like rules and regulations and regimentation and rigidity. Surely the fruit of the Spirit is not *that*?

No, it isn't. But order does not have to mean

rigidity. It means we are "on top of things," that by and large there is "a place for everything and everything is in its place." It is possible for things to be relaxed and flexible but still orderly. To have our lives "in order" is simply to be good stewards of the time and resources God has given us, so that we can make the best use of them with the least confusion. (I will say more about this in the chapter on self-control.)

Just now I mentioned "time" and "resources" as two areas that call for good stewardship. I picked these two on purpose. In my experience no areas of life go awry more quickly—and cause more unpeacefulness when they do—than our time and our money.

Tom, whom we met at the start of the chapter, provides an example—perhaps an extreme one—of how unpeaceful life can be when we do not control our use of time. Tom's most immediate problem is that he overcommits himself. He doesn't mean to, and he isn't trying to deceive his friends when he makes promises he can't keep. He just doesn't keep track of his commitments. Since he doesn't know how much time he has available and what portions of his time are spoken for, is it any wonder he has so many problems with it?

What Tom needs is a schedule. A fairly simple one would do. He could begin by listing his most important responsibilities in some of the basic areas of his life: family, job, church, personal, and so on. He could then note how much time, and which particular blocks of time, are usually occupied by those responsibilities. With this much information made clear, Tom would be much less inclined to suggest activities for which he has no time or to agree to do things that conflict with prior commitments.

Similarly, Don and Gloria's financial squabbles would ease considerably if they would devise a simple budget. A budget is not a taskmaster but a tool: a way of clearly reckoning how much money we have, where we must allocate portions of it, and how much is left for discretionary expenditures. Without a budget against which to measure their actual performance, Don can respond to Gloria's requests for household purchases only by consulting the current checkbook balance and giving off "bad vibes" when it appears to be too low. A great deal of peace would come into their marriage by the simple addition of a working budget.

The fruit of the Spirit is peace. We have peace with God because of the saving work of our Lord Jesus Christ. We grow in peace when we obey him and experience the blessings of fellowship with him. We also grow in peace as we learn to maintain right relationships with one another, and as we build into our own lives the personal order that makes those relationships possible.

Running the Race

The fruit of the Spirit is . . . patience.

THE POSTER IN THE GIFT SHOP was clever, colorful, and all too appropriate. "Lord, grant me patience," it read, "and I need it right away!"

I suspect that many people would insist that they were reasonably well-supplied with most of the familiar virtues. Few would readily admit to lacking goodness, for instance, or kindness. But I know of almost no one who would not admit to needing more patience, and to needing it "right away."

Slow to Anger

We have already seen that God is patient. When he described himself to Moses on Mount Sinai, God said he was "slow to anger" (Ex 34:6). The book of Proverbs repeatedly urges this same quality upon us:

> He who is slow to anger has great understanding,
> but he who has a hasty temper exalts folly.
> (14:29)

A hot-tempered man stirs up strife,
   but he who is slow to anger quiets contention.
                                              (15:18)

He who is slow to anger is better than the
   mighty,
   and he who rules his spirit than he who takes
   a city. (16:32)

Good sense makes a man slow to anger,
   and it is his glory to overlook an offense.
                                              (19:11)

All this sounds like excellent advice, but what
does it mean? Whether a person is "slow to anger"
might seem to depend primarily upon his or her
emotional makeup. Some of us have a long fuse
and some of us a short fuse, and those unfortunate
enough to have drawn the shorter fuses are just
going to run into more problems than everyone
else.

Actually, our situation is not so predetermined.
As with the other qualities listed as the "fruit of
the Spirit," patience is something we can grow in.
And, as with the other qualities, that growth will
take place as we see what patience looks like in the
character of Jesus and as we consciously model
ourselves after him.

The Hebrew expression that the Old Testament
translates "slow to anger" is represented in the
New Testament by two Greek words. *Makrothumia* is usually translated "patience" or "longsuffering." *Hupomone* is usually rendered

"endurance" or "perseverance." The two terms are fairly similar in meaning: both describe the virtue that enables us to cope successfully with situations that don't go the way we want them to. (Since life rarely *does* go the way we want, it is no wonder that this virtue is in such great demand.) They are not quite the same, however, and by discussing them separately we can learn a great deal about what it means to become "patient."

Calm Determination

The Greek word *makrothumia* literally means "great-tempered." It is the opposite of "short-tempered," impatient, easily frustrated. In general, it means the capacity to stick with things and not to be derailed by adversity.

In his letter to Timothy, Paul uses this word to describe the way Jesus approaches sinners:

> The saying is sure and worthy of full acceptance, that Christ Jesus came into the world to save sinners. And I am the foremost of sinners; but I received mercy for this reason, that in me, as the foremost, Jesus Christ might display his perfect patience for an example to those who were to believe in him for eternal life.
>
> (1 Tm 1:15-16)

Jesus, Paul says, is patient. Patience is part of the way he relates to sinful men and women. He desires to save them; he works to save them; and he sticks with them out of that desire until he *does* save them, or until they finally reject him. Men and women who experience conversion or a reawakening of their faith often notice, in hindsight, the careful, persistent way the Lord has worked to bring them to himself. Situations, circumstances and conversations that at the time seemed to have no particular significance clearly appear, in retrospect, to fit into an overall plan that repeatedly asserted itself in the face of their rebelliousness, and that brought them safely home in the end.

We tend to think of patience essentially as a passive quality: the capacity to "put up with it" when everything goes wrong. The dictionary bears out this notion, defining patience as "bearing pains and trials calmly or without complaint." But biblical patience is not passive; it is active, even aggressive. I like to translate *makrothumia* as "calm determination."

An interesting illustration of "calm determination" is provided by James' description of the farmer:

> Be patient, therefore, brethren, until the coming of the Lord. Behold, the farmer waits for the precious fruit of the earth, being patient over it until it receives the early and the late rain. You also be patient. Establish your hearts, for the coming of the Lord is at hand. (Jas 5:7-8)

When I was a little boy, my mother once gave me some carrot seeds to plant in a corner of the family garden. Excitedly, I opened a small furrow in the soil, placed the seeds carefully in a row, covered over the furrow with fresh soil, watered the area, and waited. All through lunch I could scarcely contain myself, as I thought about eating "my" carrots for supper. The only problem was that I was expecting to eat them for supper that same night! You can imagine my discouragement when I found out that it would take weeks before they would be ready for picking. I am sorry to report that the seeds I planted never did reach maturity, falling victim to a rather thorough neglect on my part.

Clearly, I lacked patience. But the kind of patience I needed involved more than just waiting. Every farmer knows that a successful harvest demands hard work. There is a long period between planting and harvesting, when the farmer must indeed "wait for the early and the late rain." But he does a lot more than "just wait." He weeds. He waters. He fertilizes. He expends a great deal of energy without seeing a lot of immediate results. That is what it means to be patient: to stick with something, to see it through, even when the lack of immediate visible results tempts us to become frustrated.

Intercessory prayer is an area where we can easily become discouraged if we lack patience. Sometimes we pray for relatively short-term concerns, where results are immediately obvious. Often, though, we are called to intercede for situations of much greater magnitude, where the results of our prayer may be so small and so slow that they are almost imperceptible—at least to us. This is where patience comes in. Our job is to calmly and determinedly stick with our prayer, trusting God for the harvest in good time.

Another area in which patience is especially important is in our relationships with others. Paul frequently reminds his fellow Christian leaders of this:

> Preach the word, be urgent in season and out of season, convince, rebuke, and exhort, be unfailing in patience and in teaching. (2 Tm 4:2)

> And we exhort you, brethren, admonish the idlers, encourage the fainthearted, help the weak, be patient with them all. (1 Thes 5:14)

We need patience when we are trying to teach people things, whether at school, at work, or at home. If we always expect people to "get it right the first time," we will only become frustrated and disappointed. A friend of mine once spent a few days as a substitute school teacher. The teacher for whom he was substituting repeatedly urged him to repeat each day's homework assignment at least three times. My friend was skeptical. "They're supposed to be intelligent kids," he said to the teacher. "They ought to be able to remember the assignment without being badgered about it."

The teacher's reply was a study in applied patience. "As much as you and I might wish it were otherwise," he said, "my experience tells me that human beings just don't work that way all the time. I've found that if I really want them to get the assignment, it pays to repeat it a few times."

Patience is probably in greatest demand among parents and others responsible for raising children. How many times have you heard parents wonder whether they are doing the right things and, if so, why the results seem so meager? The fact is that human beings take a long time to develop. There is often quite a gap between the time that the input gets put in and the time that the outcome comes out! I have frequently heard parents of older children sit back and sigh with relief, "You know, there were plenty of times when I wondered whether everything I said and did was having any effect. It's only now, when my children are grown, that I see the results of a lot of my effort. Some things just take time, I guess. I'm sure glad I stuck with it."

Such are the fruits of patience.

Perseverance

The other Greek word that translates the Hebrew expression for "slow to anger" is *hupomone*. In most English Bibles it is rendered "endurance," though some versions translate it "steadfastness," "standing firm," "fortitude," or, illustrating its similarity to *makrothumos*, simply as "patience." Its meaning is evident in the following passage from the letter to the Hebrews:

Therefore, since we are surrounded by so great a cloud of witnesses, let us also lay aside every weight, and sin which clings so closely, and let us run with perseverance [*hupomone*] the race that is set before us, looking to Jesus the pioneer and perfecter of our faith, who for the joy that was set before him endured the cross, despising the shame, and is seated at the right hand of the throne of God. (Heb 12:1-3)

When I was in high school, for reasons that escape me even now, I decided to work out with the cross-country track team. I was not then, and am not now, a very good runner; I joined the team hoping to get some exercise, and the coach didn't seem to mind if I worked out with the team as long as I didn't bother the *real* runners.

Once, as I wheezed my way across the finish line at the end of the usual two-mile race, the coach congratulated me: "Way to go, John! You finished!" At first I thought he was being sarcastic. But he was sincere; he knew what an accomplishment it was for me to complete a race without slowing down or stopping to rest along the way. And he said something to me that I have never forgotten: "You know, you can finish a race and not win—but you'll never win if you don't finish."

How true that is, in life as well as in running! How often do we face difficulties or challenging circumstances and fail, not because we truly get beat, but because we don't finish, because we give up too soon? How often do we sin, not because temptation really and truly overpowers us, but simply because we give in to it?

The writer of Hebrews calls us to run the race of life with perseverance, and he tells us to model ourselves on Jesus. Surely Jesus is the epitome of someone who saw a job through to completion, enduring the pain and humiliation of the cross, until he could say as he died, "It is *finished.*"

Enemies of Endurance

In Hebrews 10:36 we read, "For you have need of endurance, so that you may do the will of God and receive what is promised." What are some of the circumstances in which we especially "have need of endurance"? The letter to the Hebrews, in pointing us to Jesus as our model of endurance, mentions two important ones: "Consider him who endured from sinners such hostility against himself, so that you may not grow *weary* or *fainthearted*" (Heb 12:3).

Weariness. Paul wrote to the Galatians, "And let us not grow weary in well-doing, for in due season we shall reap, if we do not lose heart" (Gal 6:9). Weariness has to do with persevering in the day-in, day-out responsibilities of life.

Have you ever grown weary of being a Christian? I have. It can take a lot of effort. You have to pray and read the Bible regularly, and bundle the kids off to church services and prayer meetings and fellowship groups several times a week, and do the right thing when a little shortcut would be so much easier, and be nice to people who are hard to get along with—sometimes I feel like taking a month off! We have need of endurance to outlast our weariness and enjoy the refreshment of the Holy Spirit that God has waiting for us.

Faintheartedness. Weariness has to do with being ground down by the routine demands of daily life; faintheartedness has to do with facing more serious obstacles and crises that confront us from time to time. For instance, struggling to make your income cover your expenses might make you weary, but getting laid off from your job could easily make you fainthearted!

All of us find ourselves faced with intimidating obstacles at one time or another. Sometimes these obstacles are simply part of the human condition. But scripture also indicates that we face special problems, difficulties that come our way precisely because we are Christians, and because the world, the flesh, and the devil are singling us out for "special treatment." But whether the difficulties we are called to endure are categorized as "trials" (natural human problems), "tribulations" (more spiritually based difficulties), or even "persecutions," the important thing is that we *do* persevere through them.

Why? For two reasons. Remember Hebrews 10:36: "For you have need of endurance, so that you may *do the will of God* and *receive what is promised.*" First, we must endure so that we may do the will of God. We have talked about this already: God calls each of us to take part in building his kingdom, but we will never fulfill our call unless we stick with it even through adversity.

"You'll never win if you don't finish."

Second, and just as important, we must endure so that we may receive what is promised. Throughout the New Testament, God makes lavish promises to those who "endure to the end":

He who endures to the end will be saved.
(Mk 13:13)

By your endurance you will gain your lives.
(Lk 21:19)

To those who by patience in well-doing seek for glory and honor and immortality, he will give eternal life. (Rom 2:7)

Blessed is the man who endures trial, for when he has stood the test he will receive the crown of life which God has promised to those who love him. (Jas 1:12)

To him who conquers I will grant to eat of the tree of life, which is in the paradise of God.
(Rv 2:7)

But *how* do we persevere? How do we overcome weariness, and triumph over faintheartedness, and endure trials and tribulations and persecutions?

Remember the example of Jesus, who endured the cross "for the joy that was set before him" (Heb 12:2). Through his trial, his scourging, his crucifixion, his agonizing death, Jesus could *see* his reward ahead of him. He *knew* what the outcome of his perseverance would be. What is more, you and I can know it in the same way he did. Through faith in the promises of God, we too can have a confident expectation of "the joy that is set before us."

The Anchor of the Soul

The Bible calls this confident expectation *hope*. Paul described it in his letter to the Romans:

We know that the whole creation has been groaning together in travail until now; and not only the creation, but we ourselves, who have the first fruits of the Spirit, groan inwardly as we wait for adoption as sons, the redemption of our bodies. For in this hope we were saved. Now hope that is seen is not hope. For who hopes for what he sees? But if we hope for what we do not see, we wait for it with patience [*hupomone*—endurance, perseverance].

(Rom 8:22-25)

Knowing and believing the promises of God, we live in hope—in confident expectation—of the good things God has for us, and this hope is the basis of our perseverance. The letter to the Hebrews calls hope "a sure and steadfast anchor of the soul" (Heb 6:19). We all know how an anchor works. When it is firmly lodged, the winds may blow this way and that, the tide may rise and fall, the current may run here and there, but the boat will stay firmly in place. Hope is like that. It anchors us amidst the pressures and problems of life, so that we may hold fast in perseverance.

The fruit of the Spirit is patience. Not just an inborn tolerance for irritation, not just a willingness to be abused without complaining, but the calm determination to see things through without giving in to frustration, the perseverance to endure hardship for the sake of the hope we have in Christ. William Barclay describes biblical patience this way:

> It is not the patience which can sit down and bow its head and let things descend upon it and passively endure until the storm is past. It is the spirit which can bear things, not merely with resignation, but with blazing hope; it is not the spirit which sits statically enduring in one place, but the spirit which bears things because it knows that these things are leading to a goal of glory; it is not the patience which grimly waits for the end, but the patience which radiantly hopes for the dawn. (William Barclay, *New Testament Words* [Philadelphia: Westminster Press, 1964), p. 144.]

EIGHT

Solid as Rock

The fruit of the Spirit is . . . faithfulness.

NEXT TO HIS LOVE, the quality in God that scripture extols most insistently is his faithfulness.

> I will sing of thy steadfast love, O Lord, for ever;
> with my mouth I will proclaim thy faithfulness to all generations.
> For thy steadfast love was established for ever, thy faithfulness is firm as the heavens.
>
> (Ps 89:1-2)

> For God alone my soul waits in silence,
> for my hope is from him.
> He only is my rock and my salvation,
> my fortress; I shall not be shaken.
> On God rests my deliverance and my honor;
> my mighty rock, my refuge is God.
>
> (Ps 62:5-7)

Here as elsewhere, the Bible likens God to a rock. This may seem an odd, and not altogether flattering, comparison. Yet scripture says that to be faithful is to be rock-like.

Picture an enormous boulder, lodged in a field. It's solid. It doesn't change. It doesn't move. You can go away for years, and when you come back it will still be right where it was, and look exactly as it did, when you went away. Or think of bedrock: the massive layer of rock beneath the earth's outer surface. The upper layers of soil can shift and settle, but the bedrock is secure. You can build on it. The foundations of large structures are always sunk "down to bedrock." Otherwise the building will never be secure.

That is what God is like. He is like rock. He is solid, unmoveable, unchanging. You can count on him. You can build your whole life on him, confident that your foundation rests on bedrock.

The New Testament describes Jesus, too, as faithful.

> Consider Jesus, the apostle and high priest of our confession. He was faithful to him who appointed him, just as Moses also was faithful in God's house. . . . Now Moses was faithful in all God's house as a servant . . . but Christ was faithful over God's house as a son.
>
> (Heb 3:1-2, 5, 6)

The most prized quality in a servant—especially the chief steward, to which Moses is likened in this passage—was faithfulness. Intelligence, diligence, competence, respectfulness: all these were necessary as well. But faithfulness—utter reliability and trustworthiness—was absolutely essential. Moses was faithful in this way, the passage says, and Jesus far surpassed even Moses. *He* was faithful as a son, with the loyalty and dedication only an heir to the master's household would possess.

We, too, are to be faithful. We can understand faithfulness as a character trait under two main headings: reliability and loyalty.

Reliability. Like God, we are to be men and women who are "rock-like." We are to be reliable, dependable, worthy of other people's confidence. A television ad proclaims that a particular delivery service is the one to call when your package "absolutely, positively, *has* to be there overnight." We should be like that, the kind of people who can "absolutely, positively" be counted on.

Reliability is expressed in numerous ways.

Dependability. First, to be reliable means that we are people who can be entrusted with responsibility. Every employer, every supervisor, every foreman will tell you that some of their employees, if you give them an important job, may or many not do it properly and on time, while others will always come through. The ones who can be trusted are the ones who will receive both more honor and more responsibility. Jesus himself described the principle, again using the metaphor of the chief steward of a large household:

Who then is the faithful and wise servant, whom his master has set over his household, to

give them their food at the proper time? Blessed
is that servant whom his master when he comes
will find so doing. Truly, I say to you, he will set
him over all his possessions. (Mt 24:45-47)

Honesty. Employers will also tell you that many
employees are not only unreliable; they are down-
right dishonest. A few years ago I was working as a
reporter and was assigned to write a story on
Christmas-season shoplifting at a local shopping
mall. I was given a fascinating tour of one large
store's security system: two-way mirrors, plain-
clothes agents patrolling the store in the guise of
regular shoppers, even sophisticated TV monitor-
ing systems controlled from a space-age central
console in the basement.

The most surprising thing I learned, however,
was that this particular store aimed most of its
security devices at its own employees. Most stores
wouldn't admit it too readily, according to the
security guard I interviewed, but more than three-
quarters of what is euphemistically referred to as
"shrinkage" in the average department store is
due to stealing by store employees.

The Christian community to which I belong has
established a very good reputation with local
merchants and employers, who have learned that
Christians are dependable and honest workers.
We sometimes receive phone calls from local
employers asking if we can recommend people for
job openings. Christians can give a strong testi-

mony to the world by the simple practice of faithfulness and honesty.

Integrity. Reliability means we are people whose word is good. Hebrews 11 recounts the stories of men and women who have lived by faith, including Abraham's wife Sarah, who "by faith . . . received power to conceive, even when she was past the age, since she considered him faithful who had promised" (Heb 11:11). Sarah had experienced enough of God's faithfulness to know that his word was good. Can other people say the same about us?

I read a novel once that illustrated the importance of this quality in a striking way. The novel revolved around a successful politician, the mayor of a large city. Prior to his reelection campaign, he began to consider which political lieutenants he should assign to particular campaign responsibilities. One of his aides suggested a man who had worked for the mayor for many years in one of the city's precincts. He was experienced, the aide said, and people seemed to like him; perhaps he was ready to move up. "No," the mayor said. "Can't use him. I mean, I *like* him. He's a nice guy. But the man has no word, no word at all."

The man has no word. For all his experience, for all his attractive qualities, this man was of no use when important jobs were at stake because he could not be counted on to keep his commitments.

The notion of a person's "word" being "good"

calls to mind an earlier, simpler culture—the phrase itself is familiar to us mainly from movies about cowboys or farmers or small-town folks in "the olden days." But it is a very up-to-date virtue, though one in short supply in our modern culture. We should be people who are thoughtful and responsible about *making* commitments, and utterly reliable about *fulfilling* them when we do make them. We should be people who follow up, who do what we've said, and who do it properly and on time. Whole areas of life are founded upon our willingness and ability to make and keep promises: marriage, for example, or the religious life.

Our culture so ardently celebrates "freedom" and "independence" and so exalts the notion of "not getting tied down" that it takes real effort for us to learn to practice faithfulness ourselves and to pass it on to our children. If parents are casual about making and breaking promises to their children, it is unlikely that the children will learn to be faithful. Children learn first and foremost from the parents what it means to be faithful and what it means that God is faithful.

I learned this lesson the hard way once with my oldest daughter. Like all children, Sarah loves ice cream (she takes after her father in this respect). For several days she had asked me, politely but persistently, whether she and Daddy couldn't go out for an ice cream cone. I was busy and distracted and tired, and kept assuring her that we would indeed go out for ice cream together, "some day."

This worked for a while. But before long my promise of getting ice cream "some day" began to elicit the question, "But *when*, Daddy?" Finally, with a sort of magnanimous exasperation, I said, "Tomorrow."

"Really?" she asked, her eyes widening. "You promise?"

"I promise," I said. "Tomorrow night, right after dinner, you and I will go to the ice cream parlor and get an ice cream cone."

I must admit I was feeling pleased with myself. I had finally answered my little girl's question and wouldn't be pestered anymore; I got to play the part of the generous, fun-loving Dad; and besides, as I mentioned before, I *do* like ice cream.

It was then that my wife approached me. "You remember, don't you, that tomorrow night is the Super Bowl game?"

"Oh. Yes. Of course," I gulped. "Well, I can always watch the second half. . . ."

No doubt we will face situations where something more significant than a trip to the ice cream parlor is riding on our faithfulness. But that is precisely the point. Faithfulness is a full-time requirement. It won't do to keep our word only when we feel like it, or when we think it is "really important." It is *always* important to be reliable and responsible in making and keeping commitments. That is what it means to exhibit reliability, not merely as a sporadic bit of good behavior, but as an enduring character trait.

Loyalty. The other element of faithfulness is loyalty. Loyalty is a much abused concept. Many of us, when we hear the word, automatically insert the word "blind" or "uncritical" in front of it. It is unfortunately true that many wrong actions have been justified by appealing to "loyalty"—to one's employer, one's superior officer, one's country. Even when loyalty is not associated with some embarrassing misdeed, it suggests a kind of personal subordination that modern people find distasteful.

Actually, loyalty simply means faithfulness in relationships. It means that we do not let difficulties or inconveniences call into question a committed relationship that we have with another person. It may be that our connection with a particular individual or group causes us embarrassment, even persecution. It may even be that someone to whom we are committed is in the wrong: in such a case, loyalty demands that we seek to right what is wrong, but without renouncing the relationship and without turning our back on the other person.

The obvious example, of course, is God's relationship with his people. Israel's infidelities repeatedly brought God's name into disrepute among the surrounding nations. But having chosen the Jews, God stood by them. The Lord punished them for their sin but did not abandon them. The Israelites may frequently have been a "stiff-necked" people, but they were always God's people.

Jesus, too, is loyal. Surely the sins and failings of his body, the church, the people called by his own name, must be acutely embarrassing to him. "For, as it is written, 'The name of God is blasphemed among the Gentiles because of you' " (Rom 2:24). Even so, as Paul reminded Timothy, "If we are faithless, he remains faithful—for he cannot deny himself" (2 Tm 2:13). God's love, especially his forgiveness, is an expression of his loyalty to his people. Having given his Son for us, having called us to himself, having adopted us as his sons and daughters, the Lord never abandons us. Like the Israelites, we are frequently a stiff-necked people, but we always remain his children. And Jesus, our brother, cannot be other than loyal, Paul says; loyalty is part of his nature. As we grow to maturity in the Holy Spirit, loyalty must increasingly become part of our character as well.

What does it mean for us to be loyal? For one thing, loyalty means standing by those to whom we are committed, supporting them when they are in need. A man I know lost his job a few years ago as a result of wrongdoing on his part. The embarrassment he suffered and the practical difficulties he encountered in rectifying his actions and starting over in a new career were bad enough. Especially discouraging was the behavior of some of his co-workers and neighbors, who suddenly stopped associating with him. Apparently none of them wanted to be known as his friend. By contrast, the loyalty displayed by his wife and the friends who stood by him and helped him back on his feet was all the more impressive.

A friend of mine once related a more mundane example of loyalty involving one of his sons. It seems the neighbor's picture window had fallen victim to a BB gun pellet. My friend is the father of six active boys, and the evidence was rather persuasive that one of them was the culprit. The neighbor, understandably upset, was *sure* my friend's son was to blame and was insistent about seeing the boy punished immediately.

"Now just a minute," my friend replied. "You may be right; in fact it seems pretty clear that you are. But I owe it to my son to ask him what happened. If he's done something wrong, you can bet I'll get to the bottom of it and see that he makes it right; but either way it's primarily a matter between my son and me."

As it turned out, my friend's son was guilty; he got a licking and had to replace the window out of money he had earned. But his father had been loyal to him: instead of simply believing the neighbor's story and acting hastily to punish his son, he stood by him, made sure he got a fair hearing, and then made sure he was punished and made proper restitution for his wrongdoing.

This story illustrates another element of loyalty: we should defend those to whom we are committed when they are not present. I am sure all of us have had the experience of hearing a friend or co-worker or relative criticized unfairly in their absence. How do we respond? Do we listen to the accusations in silence, thereby lending our tacit agreement to them? Do we simply walk away and wish we hadn't heard? One way to be loyal in such a situation is simply to say, "Wait a minute. So-and-so is a good friend of mine. I know he's not perfect, but I don't see much point in criticizing him when he's not here to tell his side of the story."

It's not hard to see that loyalty requires courage. We need to be willing to risk a little embarrassment. Sometimes we need to risk even more. The most important relationship in which to be loyal is our relationship with the Lord. The Lord takes a lot of abuse from people; "sticking up for him" in conversations can open us to ridicule. The Bible warns us that there will be times when some of us will encounter open opposition and persecution for being followers of Christ.

That is what Peter faced when Jesus was arrested. Peter renounced his relationship with the Lord rather than remain loyal and subject himself to possible arrest and persecution. Jesus later forgave him and restored their relationship. But our call is to be loyal to our Lord, to stand by him whatever the consequences to ourselves. That is why loyalty is sometimes called "the martyr virtue." It is the particular strength of character that enables us to endure trials and persecutions for the sake of Christ.

Do not fear what you are about to suffer. Behold, the devil is about to throw some of you into prison, that you may be tested, and for ten days you will have tribulation. Be faithful unto death, and I will give you the crown of life.

(Rv 2:10)

The fruit of the Spirit is faithfulness. As we grow to maturity as children of God, the Holy Spirit wants to make us men and women who stand firm in their convictions, in their responsibilities, in their relationships. He wants us to become, like God himself, unmoveable, unchanging—solid as rock.

NINE

Strength to Serve

The fruit of the Spirit is . . . meekness.

MEEKNESS IS UNDOUBTEDLY the most misunderstood of all the qualities listed by Paul as the fruit of the Spirit. Earlier, I remarked that most people would freely admit their need for more patience. I suspect that exactly the opposite is true when it comes to meekness. You have probably never heard anyone say that he wanted to become meek.

It is not hard to see why. In our culture, "meekness" has come to mean "weakness." It means being spineless or timid. Actually, though, meekness has to do with *strength*. In fact, one way to define meekness is to say that it is "strength under control." Think of a carpenter driving a nail into a board. He must use his strength, of course, or the nail will never go in. But he must keep his strength under control. If he flails away wildly with the hammer he will cause damage, and will likely miss the nail altogether. You may never have thought of driving a nail as an example of meekness, but it is: strength under control.

To grasp the true meaning of meekness, we will

consider the way that Jesus exhibited meekness as a servant, as well as some of the qualities that comprise biblical meekness, and the way in which meekness relates to its counterpart virtue, zeal.

The Great Reversal

At that time the disciples came to Jesus, saying, "Who is the greatest in the kingdom of heaven?" And calling to him a child, he put him in the midst of them, and said, "Truly, I say to you, unless you turn and become like children, you will never enter the kingdom of heaven. Whoever humbles himself like this child, he is the greatest in the kingdom of heaven".

(Mt 18:1-4)

I do not know what answer the disciples were expecting when they asked Jesus to define greatness, but I am sure they were surprised by the answers they got. Their idea of greatness was probably not much different from what ours might be: power, influence, position, wealth, triumph in battle. Jesus' response points in an entirely different direction.

It is important to understand what he is saying. When modern minds hear the words "become like children," all sorts of silly ideas pop into them. We begin to equate childlikeness with qualities like charm, innocence, simplicity of heart, or whatever other virtues we imagine children to have. Now, I do not want to demean children—I have four delightful ones of my own—but surely we know better than this. Children *do* sometimes exhibit the attractive qualities I just mentioned. But they also exhibit other traits that are not so praise-worthy: selfishness, willfulness, independence, stubborness, to name just a few. My wife and I have often marvelled at how much time and energy it takes to teach our infant children to say "please" and "thank you," compared to their almost effortless mastery of "mine!" and "no!"

When Jesus tells us to "become like children," he does not mean that we should *act* like children. It should be clear from all we have said about growing to maturity that our goal is to become spiritual adults, not spiritual children. If we misunderstand Jesus' words, we can easily turn in the wrong direction.

Very well, then, what *did* he mean? Just this: that we should take the position that children held in Jewish society, the lowest position, the position of a servant. The disciples would have grasped this meaning immediately. Jesus was making the same point he made later by saying, "Whoever would be great among you must be your servant, and whoever would be first among you must be your slave; even as the Son of man came not to be served but to serve" (Mt 20:26-28).

Greatness, Jesus says, consists not in attaining a position in which others serve you, but in taking a position in which you serve others. He points to himself as the supreme example, as does the apostle Paul:

Do nothing from selfishness or conceit, but in humility count others better than yourselves. Let each of you look not only to his own interests, but also to the interests of others. Have this mind among yourselves, which you have in Christ Jesus, who, though he was in the form of God, did not count equality with God a thing to be grasped, but emptied himself, taking the form of a servant, being born in the likeness of men. And being found in human form he humbled himself and became obedient unto death, even death on a cross. Therefore God has highly exalted him. (Phil 2:3-9)

The full force of this passage comes home to us when we understand that the Greek word here translated "servant" is actually the word for "slave." Jesus, the Son of God, himself fully God, through, by, and for whom the world and everything in it was created, became a slave—and *therefore*, Paul says, precisely *because* he became a slave, God highly exalted him. Jesus provides the model we are to follow.

Something in us rebels at this. Everything in us and everything around us urge us to glorify ourselves, to fulfill ourselves, to avoid becoming the slave of others. Advertisements prod us to "have it our way," as if we needed encouragement, and bestselling books teach us how to "look out for number one," as if we needed to learn.

Clearly, we need to make a radical shift in our

understanding of what it means to be great, to be strong, to be meek. It is hard for us to picture God as "meek," at least in the sense in which we have come to misunderstand the word. But by looking at Jesus, we see true meekness—strength under control— expressed in true servanthood.

The Servant of All

The Hebrew word that our English Old Testament translates "meekness" is *anavah*. Literally, this word means "lowness" or "lowliness."It refers both to an objective situation—belonging to the lowest social class—and to a characteristic way of relating to people—the way a member of the lowest class would relate to those "above" him in the social order.

This Hebrew word was represented in Greek by two words, each of which reflects a different aspect of the same basic reality. *Tapeinophrosune* means "humility." It is the word used in Philippians 2:3, and concerns the estimation we hold of ourself and our position in regard to others. To be humble means to consciously consider ourselves the servant of others; thus, to "count others better than" ourselves means not to think ourselves worthless, but to count others as deserving of our service.

The other Greek word for *anavah* is *prautes*. This is the word Paul uses in Galatians 5:23. It describes the way we act as we go about serving others. Thus it might be translated "the inner

quality of relating to others as their servant."
Actually, there is no single English word that
adequately captures the meaning of *prautes*. I will
continue to use the word "meekness," despite the
misleading connotations it has for us. By examining more closely some of the qualities that go into
it, we will try to come to a fresh and more helpful
understanding of it.

Respectful. Show perfect courtesy toward all
men (Ti 3:2). The word here translated "courtesy"
could also be translated "respectfulness" or even
"meekness." This, of course, would be one of the
most immediately recognizable traits of a servant.

Respectfulness is the opposite of arrogance.
Arrogance can take different forms: sometimes it
is what we might call "hot" arrogance, characterized by an insulting, challenging, abusive
approach to others. Other times arrogance is
expressed in "coolness": being aloof and indiffer-
ent toward people. We are to be neither of these.
Rather, our approach to others should be marked
by a genuine warmth, by personal interest in
them, by courtesy and respectfulness in speech
and bearing.

Non-Defensive. A meek person is patient and
forbearing in the face of attack or abuse. He is
willing to stand up for what is right, but he places
the defense of God's honor above his own.

A good example of this aspect of meekness is
provided in the book of Numbers. Miriam and

Aaron, having become somewhat frustrated with Moses' way of doing things, murmur against him and his actions. Scripture says that Moses was "very meek, more than all men that were on the face of the earth" (Nm 12:3). God honors Moses' meekness and intervenes to silence Miriam and Aaron.

Our first reaction in such a situation might be to fight back: "Miriam and Aaron said that, did they? Boy, just wait until I get my hands on them. . . ." But Moses was able to trust the Lord for his vindication.

Being meek does not require us to be the kind of people who "take everything lying down," or who let others "walk all over" us. In one of his letters to Timothy, Paul tells his young protege to correct his opponents with gentleness" (2 Tm 2:25). What is noteworthy is that Timothy is to correct his opponents gently—or meekly—but that he *is* nevertheless to correct them. It will often be the case that in defending what is right we will also be defending ourselves, to the extent that we are in the right. Our motive, however, is not merely to defend ourselves, but to stand up for what is right.

Teachable. "Therefore put away all filthiness and rank growth of wickedness and receive with meekness the implanted word, which is able to save your souls" (Jas 1:21).

To be meek means to be the kind of person who can be taught, who can consider other points of view, who is not opinionated or rigid in insisting on his own understanding of things. He is eager to lay hold of the truth, whether it comes through God's word in scripture or through the teaching and example of others, even if it means adjusting his own point of view.

Obedient. We have already seen that Jesus, the model servant, was "obedient unto death" (Phil 2:8). It goes without saying that the prime characteristic of a servant is that he does what his master tells him.

This means that the servant seeks to meet the master's needs, not his own. Christians often fall into a trap when it comes to "Christian service." It is easy to think of service primarily as a vehicle to fulfill ourselves, to utilize our abilities. Rather than focus on what *we* most want to do, we should be thinking first of how best to serve the other person. Our call is to serve others, not ourselves.

> Come to me, all who labor and are heavy laden, and I will give you rest. Take my yoke upon you, and learn from me; for I am gentle and lowly in heart, and you will find rest for your souls. (Mt 11:28-29)

Jesus is here describing what he is like *as a master over his disciples*. Even when in a position of authority, the meek person is a servant. Christians do not exercise authority the way other people do, "lording it over" those under them. Rather, they are the servants even of those they govern.

The Source of Meekness

As we noted before, there is something in us that resists the notion of being a servant, something that protests, "Nobody's gonna push *me* around!" If we are to become meek, that "something" in us needs to be broken.

Brokenness is the source of meekness. It is a familiar word among Christians, though it is subject to misunderstanding. Watchman Nee, in his book *The Release of the Spirit,* points out that there are two very different meanings of this word. People sometimes use the expression "a broken man" to refer to someone who has been overcome by some problem and has lost the will to fight back, someone whose self-esteem has been shattered, who has simply given up on life.

The other sense of brokenness, the one that applies to the Christian life, is that of taming, or "breaking," a wild horse. Nee observes that breaking a horse doesn't rob the horse of his strength or reduce him to helplessness, but instead helps him gain control of his strength and become more useful and obedient.

To be broken, in the sense in which we are using the term, does not mean to be crushed in spirit. If we are to become useful and obedient servants of the Lord, we need to be broken the way a horse is broken, in the areas of self-will and wildness.

To be meek, we must surrender our will to the Lord and learn to give way to him and to others whenever it is right to do so. This means that, when corrected or asked to do something we would rather not, we welcome the correction or instruction meekly, rather than become hostile or irritable. It also means that we do not insist on our own preferences, our own way of doing things. This is just as important in small things as in large. Some people express complete willingness to be sent to some exotic place to serve the Lord, but at the same time insist that their toast be crisp, their soup hot, and their meat medium-rare. We should be willing to give up our preferences in order to serve the Lord and others more effectively.

What about wildness? When something unusual or unexpected happens to an untamed horse, he may become frightened and take off across the field, or he may turn and attack. Many of us are similarly hostage to our emotions: when something unexpected or unpleasant happens, we react according to how we feel rather than respond according to what we know to be right. To have our wildness broken means to be able to overcome our impulses and ask, "How should a servant of God handle this situation?"

Zeal

Chapter 21 of Matthew's gospel presents an intriguing picture of the character of Jesus. The first eleven verses recount Jesus' triumphal entry into Jerusalem, which Christians commemorate on Palm Sunday. Matthew describes the circumstances surrounding the procurement of Jesus' donkey, which took place, he explains,

> to fulfill what was spoken by the prophet, saying,
> "Tell the daughter of Zion,
> Behold, your king is coming to you,
> *humble,* and mounted on an ass,
> and on a colt, the foal of an ass". (Mt 21:4-5)

Immediately upon his arrival in the city, we see Jesus in the temple:

> And Jesus entered the temple of God and drove out all who sold and bought in the temple, and he overturned the tables of the money-changers and the seats of those who sold pigeons. He said to them, "It is written, 'My house shall be called a house of prayer'; but you make it a den of robbers". (Mt 21:12-13)

The contrast could not be more striking. One moment we see in Jesus the very picture of humility (or meekness); the next, we see him acting with an aggressiveness that is almost startling. John, describing the same incident, notes that the disciples saw in Jesus' behavior the fulfillment of another Old Testament saying: "Zeal for thy house will consume me" (Jn 2:17). Jesus, the meek king, is at the same time bold and aggressive.

We cannot properly comprehend the meaning of meekness until we see it alongside its counterpart virtue, zeal. We often equate zeal with a particular kind of personality: vibrant, enthusiastic. But that is not zeal. Zeal can be defined as "aggressive dedication." I like to describe it as "having a one-track heart." Enthusiastic people can, of course, be zealous, but so can more reserved people whose hearts are totally "sold out" for the gospel.

Scripture calls us to be zealous, to be aggressively dedicated to the Lord. "God did not give us a spirit of timidity," Paul reminded Timothy, "but a spirit of power and love and self-control" (2 Tm 1:7). Later he urges Timothy to "be strong in the grace that is in Christ Jesus" (2:1) and to fight the good fight (4:7). We are called to be meek, but we are also called, as Timothy was, to be strong, to be powerful, to be "fighters"—to be zealous.

The Right Response

When he heard there was serious sin among the Christians at Corinth, Paul wrote to them:

> Some are arrogant, as though I were not coming to you. But I will come to you soon. . . . What do you wish? Shall I come to you with a rod, or with love in a spirit of meekness?
>
> (1 Cor 4:18-19, 21)

Paul is offering the Corinthians a choice. If they repent of their sin, he will come to them in a spirit of meekness. If they arrogantly continue in their sin, he will come "with a rod"—forcefully and boldly. His position illustrates the fact that different responses are appropriate in different situations. In some cases, a Christian must be bold and aggressive. In others, it is best to be more gentle.

The key to discerning when to be aggressive and when to be gentle lies in adopting the heart of a servant. Which kind of behavior will best serve the Lord's interests in a given situation? Which kind will best serve the people involved? There are three points that can help us decide on the most appropriate response.

First, when it is our claim, our right, our way of doing something that is at stake, it is usually appropriate to be accommodating, to yield our self-will to the needs of others. When it is God's claim, God's right, God's way that is at stake, when truth and justice hang in the balance, we should be more aggressive and forceful in dealing with the situation.

The second determining factor is whether we have authority over the person or situation at hand. For example, as a father I am charged by God with the responsibility for my family and household. Therefore I can and should deal firmly with problems that arise under my roof. However, if the same problems were to arise in my neighbor's house, my response would be different, since

I do not have the responsibility or the authority to deal with them.

Finally, we can decide to take a particular approach because, after thoughtful and prayerful consideration, we think that it will be the most helpful one to take at a certain moment. Will our old friend from college respond to a bold proclamation of the gospel, or might we do better to take a low-key approach? The answers are not clear-cut; we must rely on the wisdom that the Holy Spirit gives us to discern which approach will be most fruitful.

The fruit of the Spirit is meekness. We are to be strong, aggressively dedicated Christians whose strength is channeled into serving others. Jesus, who had all power in heaven and on earth, came to us as a servant. He didn't hesitate to speak with authority, to correct, exhort, and reprove, but he always did so as one who had taken "the form of a slave." That same attitude characterizes the behavior of a truly meek Christian. Whether he is gentle or aggressive at any particular moment, he is at all times a servant, modeling himself on Jesus, the perfect servant.

TEN

The Enabling Virtue

The fruit of the Spirit is . . . self-control.

A POPULAR NOVEL from a few years back tells the story of a young man driven by the desire to be an artist. Possessed of considerable talent, he was beginning to meet with some success. His father, a godly man, was not opposed to his son's artistic endeavors, but feared that they were becoming too dominant in his life, and urged him to moderate his emphasis on art. "But don't you see?" his son replied in frustration. "I *have* to be an artist. I can't do anything but be an artist. It's the way God has made me."

His father's response was a wise one. "If you really have no control over it," he said, "then I doubt it is from God. That isn't the way God operates."

In chapter seven we discussed what it means to be a steward, to be responsible for the possessions of another. Well, we are God's possessions, and he has appointed us to be stewards over ourselves— our lives, our talents, our desires, our actions. He wants us to "rule ourselves" wisely and well on his behalf. That is what is meant by self-control. We have already read Proverbs 16:32, which highlights the importance of self-control:

> He who is slow to anger is better than the
>   mighty,
> and he who rules his spirit than he who takes
>   a city.

Even so, self-control is not an extremely popular virtue. We probably recognize our need for it, but we do so a bit grudgingly. It does not sound like much fun to be self-controlled. We think of it as the quality that makes us mow the lawn on Saturday afternoon when we would rather play tennis, the quality that restrains our more pleasurable instincts, calls us from enjoyment back to duty, prevents us, in the final analysis, from having *too* good a time.

Actually, self-control is not such a spoilsport. It is the virtue that enables us to triumph over obstacles, to conquer disabling habits, to maximize our effectiveness as servants of the Lord. True self-control—we sometimes speak of it as the ability to "be master of yourself" or to "be self-possessed"—is a source of great peace in our lives, and a doorway to tremendous spiritual growth. A Christian who has grown in self-control will be joyful and fruitful in his Christian life, not dour and inhibited.

Overcoming Obstacles

Scripture tells us we are confronted by three powerful enemies: the world, the flesh, and the

The Enabling Virtue 135

devil. The "world" is the system of unredeemed human society that works apart from, and even in opposition to, God's plan (see 1 Jn 5:19). The "flesh" refers to the "old man" within us whose habits and desires continually goad us into wrong behavior (see Rom 6:6, 7:14-25). And the "devil" is Satan himself, with the host of rebellious spirits under his command (see Eph 6:12).

> A man without self-control
>   is like a city broken into and left without walls.
>   (Prv 25:28)

The image is striking. Picture an ancient city, sacked and looted by its enemies, its wealth carried away, its people decimated. Worst of all, its walls are destroyed. It took a great army to breach the walls the first time, but now any marauding band can attack at will.

That is what we are like without self-control: we have no defense against the world, the flesh, the devil; against temptation, unruly emotions, disordered desires, addictions. We are easy prey for our enemies.

Our need for self-control is evident in a number of specific areas that commonly afflict people.

Natural Desires. God has provided us with many good things, for which we are supposed to experience a healthy desire: food and drink, sleep, and sexual pleasure are some obvious examples. But these natural desires can become unruly and overstep their bounds. We need self-control to keep them within their proper limits.

Emotions. Emotions, as we said in chapter five, were created by God and were part of what he saw when he proclaimed us "very good." It is entirely right that a child of God should experience the full range of human feelings. But, as we also said, our emotions can begin to dominate us. We either become afraid of our emotions and try to repress them, or we are tricked into believing that they alone point us to reality and ought, therefore, to be followed blindly. Anger and fear, for instance, *can* work to help us follow the Lord; instead, they often overwhelm our efforts to respond rightly in various situations. We need self-control to enable our emotions to serve us properly.

Addictions. By an addiction, I mean a craving for something that goes beyond being just an unruly natural desire and takes the form of a taskmaster. Addictions often stem from psychological or even physical dependency. It is a sign of the times we live in that many people are actually in bondage to any number of destructive behaviors. Some prominent examples include:

—Weight control. I am continually amused by the outpouring of newspaper and magazine advertisements for diet plans that promise to help people lose weight "without hunger" and without restricting their mode of eating. It may be that some weight problems are due to hormonal imbalances or to other physical causes. But far more often, overeating is an addiction, an habitual behavior learned in response to some emotional or psychological dependence. The solution is not pills but self-control, in the form of diet and exercise!

—Drink. The incidence of alcoholism in our society is frightful. One need not end up on skid row to be considered an alcoholic. "Needing" a drink every night to "wind down" from work, or to enable oneself to get to sleep, can indicate a dependence on alcohol and a need for self-control.

—Smoking. I am sure you have heard the old joke, "I can quit smoking any time I want to—I've done it dozens of times." Smoking is worse than an unpleasant habit; it is a harmful and self-destructive addiction which requires self-control if it is to be overcome.

—Masturbation. I remember being told in high school—and not quite believing it—that almost all men and many women have difficulty with masturbation at some time or other. My experience in pastoral counseling persuades me that this is true; it also persuades me that masturbation takes the form of an addiction for some. Contrary to what an overdeveloped sense of guilt might try to tell you, masturbation is not the most awful sin you can commit. It is, however, a vexing problem, and one whose solution lies mainly in the area of self-control.

Hobbies. Hobbies and outside interests are important ingredients of human life. They provide refreshment and relaxation, and can help us develop useful skills and character traits. But such interests can run amok. As a friend of mine once said, baseball is a fine diversion, but when you can identify the long-relief specialist for the Chicago Cubs and cannot identify the current President of the United States, you have gone too far. We need self-control to keep our hobbies and outside interests in proper perspective.

Speech. Much, if not most, wrongdoing is committed with the tongue. Scripture—especially the book of Proverbs—has much to say about slander, gossip, foul language, and the need to tame our tongue. James observes that anyone who can succeed in governing his speech will find self-control in other areas easy by comparison (Jas 3:2).

No doubt we could list many other areas in which self-control plays an important role. But when Paul cites self-control as the fruit of the Spirit, he is talking about something more than a corrective treatment for various specific problems. Self-control should be a quality that characterizes our life overall.

Paul notes that "every athlete exercises self-control in all things" (1 Cor 9:25). Note the last two words: *all things*. It is no surprise that an athlete exercises self-control in those things most obviously and directly related to his sport: a runner will be quite diligent about running every day; a tennis player will regularly work on his backhand stroke. But a good athlete will go beyond this. He will not merely be a disciplined runner or tennis player, but he will be a disciplined *person.* He will exercise self-control in his eating habits, sleep patterns, and use of leisure time. He will bring all his actions and habits under control, the better to advance his main goal of athletic excellence. As he does, he will grow in the basic virtue of self-control, which will carry over beneficially into his athletic pursuits.

It is the same in the Christian life. I have known Christians who tried to be very disciplined in those activities that seemed directly related to Christianity: praying for a half-hour every morning, reading two chapters from the Bible every evening, never missing church on Sunday. But because they did not employ self-control in their life more generally, they found these "spiritual disciplines" much harder to maintain. Now I am not saying we should abandon things like regular prayer and scripture reading; on the contrary, they are vital to our sustained growth in spiritual maturity. I *am* saying we will find that spiritual discipline works better when it operates in the context of a life characterized by self-control.

I call self-control "the enabling virtue" because it is the quality that makes possible our growth in all the other virtues. In each quality we have discussed as part of the fruit of the Spirit, we have seen that the Holy Spirit is its source, but that we must actively cooperate with him if we are to grow in it.

Self-control produces in us an inner confidence as we approach life, what scripture calls "strength of soul" (Ps 138:3). It makes our performance in various situations more predictable. We learn that we can trust ourselves to do the right thing in difficult situations as well as under more ordinary circumstances, and so we can face them with serenity and even with boldness.

How to Grow in Self-Control

If you are serious about growing in self-control, I would recommend taking seven basic steps. These steps can be applied to gaining self-control in a particular area, and they can also help you grow in self-control as a general character trait.

1. Desire it. This first step sounds simple enough, and it is, but it is often overlooked and sometimes difficult to take. Before you can gain self-control in a particular area, you must first want to see that area change. Many people would like to be early-risers, but when they get right down to it, they like sleeping too well to make themselves change!

2. Decide for it. Gaining self-control over a particular problem requires more than simply wishing it would happen. There is more power in deciding—in resolutely orienting your will in a particular direction—than you may realize. Overcoming a particular weakness requires a declaration of "limited war." It won't just change by itself; you are going to have to go after it consciously and deliberately.

3. Work at it wisely. Attack the problem realistically, gradually, patiently. Usually the first step is to gain an overall understanding of the problem and to devise a reasonable and comprehensive plan for overcoming it. The common mistake is to rush in with a full head of steam, attempting to eliminate the entire problem all at once.

This almost never works. Crash programs invariably crash. The result is frustration, guilt, discouragement, despair. Who has not returned from the Christmas holidays grimly determined to lose weight, embarked on a radical program of exercise and calorie reduction, and then given up after a few days, overwhelmed by the magnitude of the task? You are then worse off than when you started! It is important to have the wisdom you need in order to approach your problems sensibly and peacefully, in a manner that you can actually sustain.

4. Live in an environment of order. In chapter five we considered the importance of order in our personal life. Personal order is a major contributing factor to growing in self-control. Chaotic circumstances put unneeded pressure on areas of weakness; a peaceful and orderly environment will free you to focus your energy on the particular problem at hand.

I have often noticed that introducing order into one area of my life somehow makes it easier to gain control of other areas. For example, straightening my desk and office somehow makes it easier for me to be faithful to daily jogging. I can see no logical connection between these phenomena, other than the general principle that basic order spreads. Basic *disorder* spreads, too, and makes it that much more difficult to grow in self-control.

5. Have faith. It is especially important to exercise faith when dealing with areas that have posed significant and longstanding difficulty for you—with addictions, or with areas in which you have failed in the past. *God wants you to be free of these difficulties even more than you do.* You can and should count on him to provide the wisdom you need to attack the problem, and the strength you need to pursue your approach. Paul told the Philippians, "I can do all things in him who strengthens me" (Phil 4:13), and you can place complete confidence in that truth as well. "For God is at work in you, both to will and to work for his good pleasure" (Phil 2:13)—that is, the Holy Spirit in you gives you both the will to succeed and the strength to succeed. Decide to trust God for the strength *you* need.

6. Seek help and encouragement. You will often need the assistance of an "outside party" to help you understand your problem clearly and to set priorities, to encourage you, and to call you on when you fail. Many secular self-improvement programs have applied this principle with great success in order to help people overcome problems with drinking, overeating, smoking, and so on. It can work just as well on your problem.

7. Guard your thoughts. Resist giving in to such thoughts as "I can't do it" or "It just won't work for me." It is easy for us to become overwhelmed by the magnitude and complexity of our problems simply because we have had such a long and discouraging familiarity with them!

One of my weaknesses is to be overly analytical about my own difficulties. Fortunately, I have a friend who helps me cut through my self-imposed "paralysis of analysis." The first time he did it, I was quite shocked. I had been talking to him for some time, explaining how a particular problem worked, how I felt when I had to deal with it, the various ways I had tried to understand it, and different sophisticated solutions I had devised, when he suddenly interrupted me. "That's all very interesting," he said. "I can certainly appreciate the complexities involved. But did you ever think that the answer may be to simply *stop doing it*?"

Stop doing it! Imagine that! Somehow all my analysis had not pointed to that solution. My friend's simple advice cleared my mind wonderfully of the "There's-no-use-it'll-never-work" syndrome.

Self-control is a virtue with which it is possible to get carried away. You have probably heard of people who can wake up at any hour of the night or day without benefit of an alarm clock. I have even read of people who can, by an exercise of will power, make their own heart stop beating. Such feats are not our goal. We seek self-control, not for its own sake, but for what it can do to help us live for God.

When we talk about aggressively tackling problem areas in our life, we must also bear in mind that some problems are more important to attend to than others, and that we can't do everything at once. The Lord knows our problems and weaknesses, and he knows what it will take to overcome them. We should want to be righteous, and we should want to be in control of our lives as good stewards, but not in a way that allows anxiety to overrule grace and wisdom.

The fruit of the Spirit is self-control. With the help of the Holy Spirit, we can be men and women who overcome obstacles, conquer wrongdoing, and withstand the world, the flesh, and the devil. We really *can* do all things in him who strengthens us!

ELEVEN

Principles of Spiritual Growth

WE HAVE BEEN TALKING ABOUT what Paul calls "the fruit of the Spirit." The very word "fruit" suggests something that grows, something that starts as a seed and, with time and proper care, ripens to maturity.

It is like that with the fruit of the Spirit. This fruit—a life conformed to the character of Jesus—is not something that arrives fully developed when the Holy Spirit comes to us. Rather it *begins* then, and ripens in us as we grow to maturity as God's sons and daughters, as we live in the Holy Spirit.

Spiritual growth does not simply involve an increase in religious experience. It means growth in character, in holiness, in righteousness. It means reaching maturity as sons and daughters of God, coming to a point where God himself can be seen in us.

In this chapter we will consider four principles of spiritual growth. They are not merely "do-it-yourself" stages to self-improvement. Rather, they incorporate both the activity that the Holy Spirit already has begun in us, as well as some ways we can actively cooperate with him. I have already touched on most of the principles, in one

145

form or another, at various points in our discussion. But it is worth bringing them all together in one place, so that we can see how they fit together and learn more clearly how to become the kind of men and women that God created us to be and that Jesus redeemed us to be.

Born Anew

Having purified your souls by your obedience to the truth for a sincere love of the brethren, love one another earnestly from the heart. You have been born anew, not of perishable seed but of imperishable, through the living and abiding word of God. (1 Pt 1:22-23)

This passage is but one of many in the New Testament that speak of a "new birth." Jesus once mystified the rabbi Nicodemus by telling him that he must be born again. "That which is born of the flesh is flesh," Jesus said, "and that which is born of the Spirit is spirit" (see Jn 3:1-8). In his first letter, John speaks repeatedly of what it means to be "born of God" (1 Jn 2:29, 4:7, 5:4).

Born anew. Born again. Born of the Spirit. Born of God. This is the beginning of all spiritual growth. In order to grow in the character of Jesus, we must first have his life within us.

Consider a human child. We feed, diaper, and bathe him; later we teach and train him; in time, he becomes a full-grown adult. But the only reason all the feeding and caring and teaching works is because of the "human life principle" within that child. We can do all the same things for a little puppy (to make a rather absurd comparison), but the puppy will never grow up to be a human being. He does not have the "human life principle" within him.

It is the same with spiritual growth. We need spiritual feeding and nurture, of course, but it has its effect in us, it moves us to our ultimate goal, only because we have "God's life principle" within us, because we have been reborn in the Spirit. The first principle of spiritual growth is: *Have God's life within you.*

Behold God's Glory

> And we all, with unveiled face, beholding the glory of the Lord, are being changed into his likeness from one degree of glory to another.
>
> (2 Cor 3:18)

We grow, Paul says, as we behold God. When we are born into God's family, we gain the right of access to God's throne room. We can come into his presence, hear his word, come to know him even as we are known by him. As we do this, we are changed, degree by degree, to become more like him.

You have probably noticed how children are often "just like" their parents. Of course, they resemble them physically, because of genetic factors, but that is not primarily what I mean. I am

talking about the uncanny similarities of mannerisms, speech patterns, ways of thinking and acting,
that become evident as a child grows up. Even
more than mere physical likeness, these are the
similiarities we refer to when we say that someone
is "just like her mother," or "a chip off the old
block."

There is little wonder that these similarities
occur, considering the enormous amount of time
that children spend with their parents. Their
parents simply "rub off" on them. For the most
part, this happens of its own accord, without the
children making a conscious effort to become like
their parents. Many times they are not even aware
of how like their parents they are.

The same principle holds true in our relationship with God. The more we are "around God,"
the more we simply dwell in his presence, the
more we absorb his likeness, the more he "rubs
off" on us. In personal prayer, in corporate
worship, in scripture, in living among Christian
brothers and sisters—in all these ways we come
into God's presence, where we can behold his
glory and be changed by him. The second principle of spiritual growth is: *Dwell in God's presence.*

Imitation

Therefore be imitators of God, as beloved
children. And walk in love, as Christ loved us
and gave himself up for us, a fragrant offering
and sacrifice to God. (Eph 5:1-2)

We grow spiritually by imitating God. To a certain degree, as we just saw, he simply "rubs off" on us. But scripture calls us beyond this, to an active process of deliberately modeling ourselves on the example of God and of Jesus.

I know the word "imitate" can call to mind the old saying, "Monkey see, monkey do." That does not sound very spiritual, and it is not very flattering to us, who are cast in the role of the monkey! But flattering or not, it is the truth: we grow to be like God by imitating him.

Of course, there are some ways in which it is meaningless for us to try to imitate God. Try as we might, we cannot become infinite, or omnipotent, or omniscient.

There are also some ways of imitating Jesus that miss the point. Jesus said that he "had no place to lay his head," and so we may think we need to adopt a lifestyle of simplicity in order to be like Jesus. Jesus was a carpenter, and so we may think we need to adopt a particular occupation in order to be like Jesus. Now, there certainly is nothing wrong with a simple lifestyle or with being a carpenter, and God does call some people to those ways of life. My point is simply that these are not the *main* ways in which *all* of us are called to imitate Jesus.

Paul told the Ephesians to imitate God by walking in love (see Eph 5:1-2). This brings us closer to the main point. We are to imitate God's character, his love, his joy, his peace—you know the rest of the list by now. We understand what he is like by observing how he thinks, how he relates to people, how he responds to situations. We then grow to resemble him by doing likewise in our own circumstances.

C.S. Lewis, in his book *Mere Christianity*, describes it this way:

> You are putting yourself in the place of a son of God. To put it bluntly, you are *dressing up as Christ*. If you like, you are pretending. . . . In a way, this dressing up as Christ is a piece of outrageous cheek. But the odd thing is that he has ordered us to do it.
>
> Why? What is the good of pretending to be what you are not? Well, even on the human level, you know, there are two kinds of pretending. There is a bad kind where the pretense is there instead of the real thing; as when a man pretends to help you instead of really helping you. But there is also a good kind, where the pretense leads up to the real thing. When you are not feeling particularly friendly but know you ought to be, the best thing you can do, very often, is to put on a friendly manner and behave as if you were a nicer person than you actually are. And in a few minutes, as we all have noticed, you will be really feeling friendlier than you were. Very often the only way to get a quality in reality is to start behaving as if you had it already. . . .
>
> You see what is happening. The Christ himself, the Son of God who is man (just like

you) and God (just like his Father) is actually at
your side and is already at that moment beginning to turn your pretense into a reality. . . . He
is beginning to turn you into the same kind of
thing as himself. . . .

The third principle of spiritual growth is:
Imitate Jesus and the Father.

"This Is a Test"

Count it all joy, my brethren, when you meet
various trials, for you know that the testing of
your faith produces steadfastness. (Jas 1:2-4)

One often overlooked truth about character
traits such as the ones we have been discussing is
that we grow in them only by *using* them, and we
use them only in situations where we *need* them.

It seems to me that Christians often take just the
opposite approach. We confuse having a quality
with never needing to use it. For example, when
we pray, "Lord, grant me patience," what we
often really mean is, "Lord, preserve me from
frustrating situations." We might as well pray,
"Lord, make sure I never need patience." After
all, how will we ever grow in patience if we never
have to deal with situations that are frustrating?
That is precisely what patience is *for*.

The obvious implication—I am trying to break
this to you gently—is that growing in the fruit of
the Spirit is apt to mean more trials, not fewer, as

we grow to maturity—at least until we have shown we have learned our lesson and have successfully internalized the traits God is trying to produce in us. In the meantime, we need to be tested, to show us the progress we have made and the progress we have yet to make. God thoughtfully provides these tests at appropriate intervals.

Have you ever heard a radio station run a test of its emergency broadcast system? It begins with a somber voice intoning the words, "This is a test. . . ." God sometimes speaks to us just that way. A particular instance from my own life is etched in my memory.

It was the middle of winter, a cold, windy, snowy day. I was having "one of those days." It started with a flat tire. I tried to change it, but the lug nuts were rusted in place and I couldn't budge them. After a certain amount of wailing and gnashing of teeth, I decided there was nothing to do but try to drive the car, flat tire and all, to a nearby service station. I had driven about three blocks when I realized that the tire was slowly but surely shredding right on the wheel (one thing you are not supposed to do with a flat tire is to drive on it—I know that now). Figuring I had nothing more to lose—the tire was already ruined—I pressed on, only to discover how hard it is to make a left turn in a car that has a flat right tire. As the car rumbled, groaned, vibrated, and finally veered into a snow bank, I clearly heard the fateful words: *This is a test. . . .*

Considering that I managed to compose myself

by the time the tow truck arrived, and even to conduct a fairly jovial conversation with the driver, I think I can say that I passed this particular test. All right, there *were* my assorted mutterings and grumblings. And I did, well, sort of throw the lug wrench once. I suppose I would have to say that I just *barely* passed the test. Call it a D+.

Testing makes us stronger. Weight lifters call this "the overload principle." If you continue to work out with the same amount of weight, you will stay in shape but you will not grow stronger. The way to increase your strength is to work with about ten percent more weight than you find comfortable; your muscles will grow stronger in response to the increased load. So it is with virtue: our capacity increases as we deal successfully with trials.

For this reason, it makes sense for us to welcome, and even to seek out, fresh challenges that promise to test and strengthen us. I learned this from a high school friend, Joe Vincente. Joe and I were on the football team together. One of the drills we used to run consisted of forming two groups of linemen, facing each other, about twenty feet apart; when the whistle blew, the first man in each line ran, full tilt, directly toward the other. The object was to collide in such a way as to pulverize the opposing lineman.

In such a situation, human nature compels one to count back the appropriate number of places in the other line, in order to learn who one is about to collide with. On this particular occasion, my "partner" was to be a rather large young scholar named Jerry Bannion. Jerry had a well-deserved reputation as the toughest and meanest guy on the football team.

One by one, as the coach's whistle blew, the players ahead of me raced off to meet their fate. Finally it was my turn. I peered across at the other line. There crouched Jerry, his eyes blazing with anticipation. The coach raised the whistle to his lips. Just then, as my whole life was flashing before my eyes, my friend—my very *good* friend— Joe Vincente stepped in front of me. *I want Bannion,* he growled.

I am sure there is a special place in heaven reserved for Joe Vincente. Besides saving my neck, he taught me an important spiritual lesson. He sought out testing. He wanted to find out how strong and how brave he was, so he went after the stiffest test available. As it happened, he survived the encounter; I am sure he also grew in self-knowledge, in strength, and in courage. (I, for my part, learned a priceless lesson about *gratitude.*)

Blessed is the man who endures trial, for when he has stood the test, he will receive the crown of life which God has promised to those who love him. (Jas 1:12)

Our character is what makes us effective as Christians. This is what makes us useful to the Lord: that we can be relied upon, can be entrusted with great gifts and great responsibilities, because our character has been tested and proven.

Most of us have probably been men and women who reacted to circumstances, who sought the path of least resistance, who followed the crowd. But our call as Christians is not to take the easy course, but to take the *right* course. The Lord wants us to be people who are able to do what he calls us to do, whose character enables us to obey, to serve, to be fruitful.

We should want to be Christians who are tested and proven, who know what we are capable of, who know that we really *are* what we profess to be. The fourth principle of spiritual growth is: *Welcome testing and trials.*

The fruit of the Spirit is love, joy, peace, patience, kindness, goodness, faithfulness, meekness, self-control, and a host of other qualities too numerous to mention. The fruit of the Spirit is a life conformed to the character of Jesus Christ. By being born into God's family, we have access to such a life; by dwelling in God's presence, imitating him and his son Jesus, and embracing the tests he lays before us, we grow in likeness to him until we reach full maturity as his sons and daughters.

His divine power has granted to us all things that pertain to life and godliness, through the knowlege of him who called us to his own glory and excellence, by which he has granted to us his precious and very great promises, that through these you may escape from the corruption that is in the world because of passion, and become partakers of the divine nature. For this very reason make every effort to supplement your faith with virtue, and virtue with knowledge, and knowledge with self-control, and self-control with steadfastness, and steadfastness with godliness, and godliness with brotherly affection, and brotherly affection with love. For if these things are yours and abound, they keep you from being ineffective or unfruitful in the knowledge of our Lord Jesus Christ. Therefore, brethren, be the more zealous to confirm your call and election, for if you do this you will never fall; so there will be richly provided for you an entrance into the eternal kingdom of our Lord and Savior Jesus Christ. (2 Pt 1:3-11)

The books in the Living as a Christian series can be used effectively in groups. To receive a free copy of the Leader's Guide to this book and the others in the series, write to Servant Book Express, Box 8617, Ann Arbor, Michigan 48107.